LORI PECKHAM, editor

Guide's Greatest

NARROW ESCAPE STORIES

REVIEW AND HERALD® PUBLISHING ASSOCIATION

Since 1861 | www.reviewandherald.com

Published by Review and Herald® Publishing Association, Hagerstown, MD 21741-1119

Review and Herald® titles may be purchased in bulk for educational, business, fund-
raising, or sales promotional use. For information, please e-mail SpecialMarkets@re-
viewandherald.com.

The Review and Herald® Publishing Association publishes biblically based materials
for spiritual, physical, and mental growth and Christian discipleship.

The author assumes full responsibility for the accuracy of all facts and quotations as
cited in this book.

Unless otherwise noted, Bible texts are from the *Holy Bible, New International
Version*. Copyright © 1973, 1978, 1984, International Bible Society. Used by permission of Zondervan Bible Publishers.

This book was
Edited by Lori Peckham
Designed by Trent Truman
Cover art by Tim Jessell
Typeset: Goudy 13/16

PRINTED IN U.S.A.

12 11 10 09 08   5 4 3 2 1

Library of Congress Cataloging-in-Publication Data

Guide's greatest narrow escape stories / Lori Peckham, editor.
     p. cm.
 1. Children—Religious life—Juvenile literature. 2. Providence and government of
God—Juvenile literature. 3. Christian life—Adventist authors—Juvenile literature.
I. Peckham, Lori. II. Title: Greatest narrow escape stories.
 BV4571.3.G85 2007
 242—dc22

                                   2007025018

ISBN 978-0-8280-2040-4

Contents

Special Thanks — 6

Introduction — 7

Chapter 1: Under the Horses' Hoofs — 9
Mrs. Don Jennings / February 23, 1955

Chapter 2: Who Killed Growler? — 14
Norma Youngberg / November 2 & 9, 1955

Chapter 3: Deserted Island — 26
Kay Cherry / April 27, 1966

Chapter 4: The Drop That Saved — 37
Yvonne R. Bullock / August 3, 1966

Chapter 5: No Way Through — 40
Mary L. Anderson / March 15, 1967

Chapter 6: Caught in the Oven — 44
Bernadette Rajotte / July 31, 1968

Chapter 7: Flight to Freedom — 51
Jim Saunders / July 1, 1970

Chapter 8: Now See! — 57
Brian Sayer / January 12, 1972

Chapter 9: Stuck! — 63
Isabelle Edminster / February 23, 1972

Chapter 10: Morning Prayer — 68
Marion J. Prescott / June 21, 1972

Chapter 11: Midnight in the Supermarket   75
Thearon Staddon / September 13, 1972

Chapter 12: Terror on the Tracks   79
Diana Berry Sauerwein / January 24, 1973

Chapter 13: The Hand on the Doorknob   83
Evelyn Zytkoskee / February 7, 1973

Chapter 14: The Limp That God Sent   87
Elaine Egbert / December 18, 1974

Chapter 15: Trouble With Boastin' Is . . .   96
Gar Baybrook / August 27, 1975

Chapter 16: Jagged Rocks and a Quiet Pool   102
Dale Dunston / August 4, 1976

Chapter 17: Deadman's Mine   107
Kenn Sherwood Roe / April 26, 1978

Chapter 18: Appointment With Death   118
Maryane Myers / August 20 & 27, 1980

Chapter 19: Chet and the Super Coop Scooper   130
Maylan Schurch / August 14, 1993

Chatper 20: Voices in the Darkness   135
Jane Chase / November 25, 1995

Chapter 21: Farm Girls on the Run   141
Judy McEvoy / April 8, 2000

Chapter 22: Miracle in the Mist   145
Jonelle M. Brody / February 7, 2004

Chapter 23: Never Alone   151
Richard Edison / March 20 & 27, 2004

Also by Lori Peckham:
  Guide's Greatest Animal Stories
  Guide's Greatest Mystery Stories
  Insight Presents More Unforgettable Stories
  Jesus in My Shoes

To order, call **1-800-765-6955.**

Visit us at **www.reviewandherald.com** for information on other Review and Herald® Products.

A special thanks to the authors we were unable to locate. If anyone can provide knowledge of their current mailing address, please relay this information to Lori Peckham, in care of the Review and Herald® Publishing Association.

Special Thanks . . .

As always, special thanks to the *Guide* editors, who have valued true, life-changing stories and have printed so many powerful ones through the years. Special thanks also to Randy Fishell and Rachel Whitaker, the current *Guide* editor and assistant editor, for their suggestions of great stories to include in this volume; and to Tanya Faith, Janet Ford, and Ryan Young for preparing this manuscript.

And thank you to my parents, Lee and Ellen Tripp, who raised me to love life and chase the joy in every day, and to my husband, Kim, and our son, Reef, who are so often the source of that joy.

—Lori Peckham

"I have come that they may have life, and have it to the full"
(John 10:10).

Introduction

Most people have a narrow escape—or two, or three—in their lifetime. Maybe you've already had one. It may not have been as dramatic as most of those in this book. But still, you felt that moment of relief. That moment of exclaiming, "Whew! That was close" or of whispering, "I could have . . ."

Perhaps your narrow escape taught you a lesson: "I should have obeyed" or "I should have been more careful." Or maybe your dangerous situation was completely out of your control and you could only say, "Thank You, God. I'm glad I'm still alive."

For that is perhaps the greatest lesson in a narrow escape. That life on this planet is fragile and can be threatened in so many ways. That we should savor and make the most of every day. And that we should live for more than this world.

Jesus gave us life in the beginning, and He wants to give us eternal life. So though we may have narrow escapes on this earth—where the devil is underfoot—and though not everyone will survive every threatening situation here, Jesus has made it possible for us to make the ultimate "narrow escape." Someday we can leave this dangerous earth and escape to His wonderful heaven!

—Lori Peckham

Under the Horses' Hoofs

by Mrs. Don Jennings

The snow glistened like millions of tiny diamonds. It was nearly six feet deep, and where the snowplow had cut through, it was piled even higher. Every child who had a sled simply could not stay away from the hill, even though the temperature was eight degrees below zero.

We lived at the foot of the hill. That morning my brother, Jack, and I hurried with our chores and housework so we could have as long as possible on our sled.

As soon as Jack was finished, he gathered up some kindling wood and matches and put them on his sled. He hauled them to the top of the hill and built a fire to keep us warm.

My work took longer, but finally Mother gave me permission to leave. I had no sled, so my brother shared his with me.

He lay on his stomach on the sled, and I knelt between his knees at the back. Then down the hill we went, over ruts and bumps, our cheeks tingling and our eyes watering. "Out of the way!" we shouted. "Here we come!"

After we flew down the hill, we continued through the valley, and up another hill nearly to the top, until we could go no farther. Then we hopped off, turned around, and went back down to the foot of the hill we had started from.

That was the ideal place for coasting. The only thing that bothered us was that now and then a horse and sleigh or a car came along. And it seemed that every time a car tried to climb the hill, it got stuck halfway up and churned holes in our snow. All of us children would stop sledding and help shovel until the car could make it over the top.

My brother and I spent the whole afternoon gleefully sliding and rolling around in the snow. At the bottom of the hill was a road turning to the right, and sometimes we tried to make that turn. It was so slick that nearly always we took a rolling tumble that jarred us up against the hard snow on the side of the road. Nearly breathless, we'd stumble around trying to get ourselves back in shape for another slide down the hill.

More and more friends gathered on the hill during the afternoon. Soon there wasn't standing room around the bonfire.

The sun was beginning to set and dusk was settling in the valley when Mother called. "You can have two more slides down the hill, and then you must come in," she said. Mother never let us stay out after dark unless there was an adult on the hill to watch us.

"We'll be in as soon as we have two more slides," we called back.

We decided that we would make the first slide from one hill to the other hill, so it would be as long as possible. Down we went, shouting and laughing. Then, for our last slide, we decided that we would try to make that right-hand turn at the bottom of the hill.

Up to the top we went, stopping to warm our hands for quite a while at the fire, for we didn't want to get home too fast. Mother had said that we could have two more slides, and now we had only one left. We reasoned, therefore, that we didn't have to go in till we had had the second slide, and she hadn't said that we couldn't stand by the fire if we wanted to in between.

After a while, though, we knew that we'd stretched Mother's patience as far as was safe and that we'd better be getting home. So my brother lay on his stomach on the sled, and I got on my knees, and down we went.

When we were about to make the turn, my brother yelled, "Hang on! We're going around!" I crouched as low as I could and hung on tight.

As we got to the turn, we saw a team of horses and a sleigh right in the middle of the road! Jack pulled hard on the guider, trying to make the sled go straight instead of turning the corner. But we hit the hard-packed bank of snow on the side of the road, and instantly it turned us around back on the road.

I closed my eyes, expecting any moment to feel the hoofs of the horses crashing on my back. In a flash I realized that if we had gone home on time, as Mother had expected, we would have been perfectly safe. Now we were in sudden danger of being killed, or at least badly injured.

But in that instant the driver pulled on the reins and shouted, "Whoa! Up! Up! Up! Whoa, boy! Up! Up! Up!"

As we raced toward them, those horses reared straight up, with their front feet pawing in the air. Under those hoofs we dashed like a streak and hit the bank on the other side of the road. Then back we bounced, right under those feet again!

Finally we stopped. Jack and I rolled out from under the horses before they set their feet down.

Shaking like leaves, we got up and thanked the driver for protecting us. Then we hurried home to Mother. We didn't stop for a moment to argue whether or not we had finished our second slide.

No one could say that we had really disobeyed

Mother the night we found ourselves underneath the horses' hoofs. She had told us we could slide down the hill two more times, and that's all we did. But we had taken a lot longer to do it than Mother had intended. We had, as people say, taken advantage of her, and I guess that's just about as bad as being disobedient.

But I have always been thankful that God gave the driver strength to hold the horses and the horses strength to hold up their front feet so long. Yes, God loves and watches over us, even when we are disobedient. But we never took advantage of our mother's patience again.

2

Who Killed Growler?

by Norma Youngberg

Missy! Missy!" The Malay gardener's voice was shrill with fright. "Missy, oh, Missy! Dog . . . he die!"

I came hurrying down the stairs and followed Garyu to the backyard. Sure enough, the handsome fox terrier, Growler, was in serious trouble. He ran wildly back and forth. Even as we looked at him, his body swelled and then dropped dead.

"Poor Growler!" I said as I knelt beside the dog's body and felt it all over for wounds or injuries. There was nothing to give us any clue about the dog's strange death.

I went down to the compound gate with a sad heart. Growler and his mate, Brownie, belonged to Mrs. Mershon, the wife of the other missionary in Sandakan, British North Borneo.

I knew that Mrs. Mershon would soon be coming home. I waited for her at the foot of the hill by the big gate. "Growler is dead!" I said to her as she came in a few minutes later.

"What killed him?" she asked, startled and full of grief.

"We don't know," I said. "He just swelled up and fell over dead." It all seemed weird and unreal.

Mrs. Mershon hurried up the hill to the house and went out to look at her dead pet. "Poison," she declared. "This is certainly poisoning. These thieving rascals always poison the dogs when they intend to rob a house."

"Do you think someone is planning to rob this house?" I asked.

"Of course!" she insisted. "You wait and see. They'll try to get Brownie, too. We must keep all the doors locked at night."

Mrs. Mershon told Garyu to dig a grave down in the canyon and bury Growler. Then she and I turned back to the house with troubled hearts.

The Mershons had been in Borneo for some time, but my husband, Gus, and I had just arrived from America with our two toddlers. We were young and inexperienced. We knew little of the language and the customs of the people among whom we had come to work.

We found this affair of the poisoned dog very disturbing. Suppose the poisoners decided to leave some tainted bits of food around where our children could find them. Ruth was 3 years old and a very active little girl. Robert was a year old and spent hours toddling and crawling all over the big house.

"I'm going to hire a jaga," Mrs. Mershon said the next morning.

She and I and the children were alone on the mission station, for our husbands had left on a tour a few days before.

"What will the jaga do?" I inquired.

"Oh, he will come at sundown and walk around the house all night so the robbers can't get in." Mrs. Mershon was pleased with the plan, and we both felt better that evening when a tall Bengali police officer came striding up the front drive.

He really did march around the house all night. He also coughed loudly under every bedroom window so we'd be sure to know that he was awake and on the job. No one could sleep very much.

The following morning, very early, everyone was awakened by a shrill, high-pitched bark from Brownie. There was something absolutely chilling about the sound, and I felt shivers run up and down my spine. I ran to the window and looked out. There in the drain at the side of the house was Brownie, twitching and struggling in convulsion.

Mrs. Mershon had also heard the wild barking

and came running. "Poor little Brownie!" she cried, lifting her pet from the wet drain and carrying her into the kitchen.

In the midst of the excitement over Brownie, our husbands returned from their trip. They had just gotten off the ship and were full of good news about their journey to the churches. But we were too upset to listen to them. Brownie was the center of attention.

"She will probably die," Pastor Mershon said as he went to look at Brownie's four little puppies snuggled in a padded basket in the Mershons' dining room.

Mrs. Mershon told the men the story as she worked over the suffering animal. "You see," she concluded, "they poisoned poor old Growler, and now they have done their best to get rid of Brownie, too."

"What about that jaga you hired to watch the house?" I asked. "Wouldn't he have seen the poisoners when they came prowling around?"

"Oh, I don't know." Mrs. Mershon was almost in tears. "I just don't trust anyone. Where did that jaga go, anyhow? I didn't see him around anywhere this morning."

"He would leave at sunrise," her husband reminded her. "Maybe the jaga was in cahoots with the thief. How do we know?"

So fear and distress filled the big mission house, and we did not allow little Ruth and Robert to go outside. Brownie began to feel a little better by noon, but it was several days before she had recovered to her usual good spirits. The jaga was told not to come back, since the missionary men were home. But no one knew when another attempt would be made to get Brownie out of the way.

The mission house was a large two-story building built like a duplex. Both sides were alike. Each side had a kitchen, a dining room, and a bathroom downstairs, and in the center was a large reception hall with a wide, open stairway leading up to the sleeping rooms and spacious upstairs veranda.

There was a double landing at the foot of the stairs, so it could be approached from the back door as well as the front. There were three steps up to the landing on both the back door and front door sides. Little Ruth and Robert loved to play on this spot. They climbed up and over and down, up and over and down, laughing and shouting as they played. Since they couldn't go outdoors to play anymore, they enjoyed hours of fun on the stair landing.

The mission house was not like any other house in Sandakan. It had been built by an American and had been used as the American consulate for some years. The builder had made this house with double walls throughout. But in the tropics only one wall was usually used, so that coolness could enter freely. Perhaps the American had realized his mistake before the house was finished. For in order to have some sort of ventilation, he had decided to leave an open space of several inches at the bottom of the walls.

The floor was a cement slab laid right on the ground. So this open space between the walls made it possible for small animals, rats, mice, and lizards to roam in and out at their pleasure. Some of these creatures found the double walls a convenient place for permanent living quarters, and it was difficult to get rid of them.

The space between the wall and the floor was too small for Brownie to crawl through, but the doors had always been open so she could go in and out. Now the doors remained closed, so Brownie and the pups had to stay inside.

One evening my husband and I were alone in the big mission house. The Mershons had gone on a trip. Suddenly we heard Brownie whining in the dining room.

"We'll have to go down there and see what's happening!" Gus exclaimed, grabbing his flashlight and starting for the stairs.

I took one reassuring look at our two sleeping babies and followed him, locking the door behind me as I left.

Electricity had just been installed in the city of Sandakan, but it was not yet properly regulated. So often the lights would dim for no apparent reason, until only the glowing wire could be seen inside the bulbs—then, after a few seconds, the bulbs would brighten again.

Gus turned on the electric light in the dining room, where Brownie and her puppies were confined. There was nothing to be seen except the puppies stirring in their basket—and Brownie, nose pointed toward the inner wall of the room, uttering her wild cries of distress. But wait! There was something to be heard. An awful snoring sound came from under the wall. It was filled with such menace that both Gus and I stopped and looked at each other, unable to speak.

The wall was about six inches above the floor at the spot from which the frightful noise issued. The Mershons' bathroom was on the other side of that wall. A private inner stairway came down into the bathroom.

Gus kneeled down and directed the beam of his flashlight under the wall. Two small bright spots caught the gleam of the light and flung it back like fierce points of fury.

"There's a snake under there!" Gus said as he scrambled to his feet.

I climbed onto the wide ledge of the open window. "O-o-o-h! Do you think it will come out?"

"I hope so!" Gus said as he hurried outside and returned with a big bamboo pole. He aimed the sharp end of the pole at the two bright spots and rammed with all his strength, but the bamboo slid among those slippery coils. The hissing and blowing increased to a hideous racket.

"Here, take Brownie and the pups upstairs!" Gus commanded.

As I carried them up, I thought briefly of the Mershons asleep on the boat sailing out of Sandakan harbor. Oh, if they could only know the wild adventure that was filling their quiet dining room that night! I examined Brownie and the pups. They appeared uninjured and much relieved to be out of sight and hearing of that horrible thing under the wall of the dining room.

I hurried back downstairs and saw that Garyu had arrived with a number of other men. They took turns prodding and pushing with the bamboo until the hooded head of a giant black cobra darted from under the wall. The great snake slithered across the room into the hall and through our dining room, where it escaped under the wall.

Still the frightful noises continued. The group in the dining room looked at one another in complete terror and surprise.

"There is another one in there!" Gus said.

"There are two or three!" Garyu had knelt down and was peering under the wall. "I can't see them anymore. I guess they have a den under there!"

"Probably a hole under the cement," someone else ventured.

"In that case, we'll have to break up the cement floor in the bathroom and clean them out of their den." Gus had no intention of fostering a den of cobras in the house where his two little children played every day.

So mallets were brought, and a few whacks on the cement floor of the bathroom showed plainly that there was a hollow place underneath it. When the cement was broken up and removed, a deep hole appeared right at the foot of the narrow stairs leading into the bathroom. The snakes had retreated into the hole, but their terrible voices could still be heard as they hissed and blew with that dreadful snoring sound.

"The snake—he blow poison," Garyu informed them. "He make plenty dead! Blow poison!"

So this was the mysterious poisoner that had killed Growler and had almost killed Brownie. The snakes had blown their deadly poison down the dogs' throats. Spitting cobras, that's what they were. We had heard of them but had never expected to have any of them as houseguests.

By this time a large crowd had gathered. The door and window of the bathroom were full of eager faces burning with curiosity about the nest of snakes under the White man's house and wondering what sort of magic he would use to get rid of them.

"Better get a gun and shoot them!" one helpful person suggested.

"We might have to get them out of the hole first," Gus said. "No one can shoot them down in that hole."

Clutching a short club, Garyu stood over the hole in the floor. "I will bring them out," he shouted. "I will bring them out!" He rammed the club down into the hole again and again, screaming terrible oaths and calling the snakes by many bad names.

I had gone upstairs to see if Ruth and Robert were still sleeping through all the tumult going on downstairs. It was now 2:00 in the morning. I returned and waited on the landing six steps above the spot where Garyu was daring the snakes to come out.

The crowd outside pressed in until the small room was filled. "What a brave man!" they exclaimed to one another. "How daring!"

These words of praise made Garyu more determined to bring out the snakes, and he lifted the club and rammed it into the hole again. All this time the dreadful noises of the snakes mingled with the threatening shouts of Garyu.

Just as the Malay lifted his club high to give it a strong downward thrust, the light dimmed until the bright wires glowed faintly in the electric bulb. A dark streak shot from the hole, and Garyu gave a loud cry. "I die! I die!"

All the onlookers fell back in terror. Gus caught him up in his arms and held him up. I ran down the six steps, took hold of the dying man, and dragged him up to the landing.

"Where? Where?" I demanded. "Where did the snake bite you?"

The tormented man raised his hand to his right eye and cried, "The other one too!"

Then we all realized that the snake had not bitten him. It had blown poison into his eyes. He was in convulsions just as the dogs had been.

The men carried him outside and laid him on the grass in the backyard. The Muhammadan Malays gathered around him. As soon as he became a little quieter, they began reminding him of his sins.

"Remember how you beat your wife last Wednesday?"

"Do you recall how you cheated Ah Sew, the vegetable man?"

"Yes, and this is what you get for your gambling and lying and stealing!"

One after another they added the torment of their rebuke to the agony in his eyes.

My husband and I did everything we knew to ease the pain. We washed his eyes with medicine until at last he felt better and everyone knew that he would not die.

Gus again turned his attention to the snakes, which were still making a noisy place of the Mershons' bathroom.

"I know what we'll do!" Gus said at last. "We have a couple bags of cement in the storeroom. We will just fill in their den with fresh cement."

So it was done without delay. A smooth floor with no holes was laid over the cobras' den. It was now almost morning. Everyone went to bed and tried to get a little sleep. Brownie and her pups were taken back to the dining room.

Late the following afternoon Garyu appeared. His eyes looked terrible, but he could see a little out of them. He brought cakes, rice, and curry. "Allow me to offer these thing to the great snakes!" he said in a meek voice. "Now I know that these are snakes by night, but by day they are powerful spirits—evil spirits with the breath of destruction in their mouths."

So the Malay made his offering to the dead snakes under the bathtub. But in the mission house that evening an offering of genuine thanksgiving was made by Gus and me to the living God in heaven. For now we knew that the cobras had been living right beside the stair landing where Ruth and Robert had spent many hours playing.

The den of the deadly cobras was actually less than two feet away. How many times the snakes and our toddlers had looked at each other will never be known. But we've always believed that guardian angels had the most important part of all in this true story of North Borneo.

3

Deserted Island

by Kay Cherry

At the sharp crackle of lightning Joe McDonald shrank back from the window where he had been sitting for the past 10 minutes. The deafening roll of thunder and the howling wind sent cold chills up his spine.

It was hard to believe that this was midmorning. The darkening clouds cast a shadow over the island, making the day appear like dusk.

"What a storm!" Joe exclaimed to himself. "Hey, Dave, come here."

"What do you want?" Dave asked. "Wow, look at that rain!"

"That's what I wanted to show you," Joe said. "Isn't it something? I've never seen it rain or blow like this before."

"Me neither. If the rain keeps up that pace much

longer, there's no telling what's going to happen."

"The radio said there's a hurricane in West Palm Beach. Do you suppose it's going to hit here?" Joe looked around nervously.

"I don't know."

"Hey, here comes Dad. He's been in hurricanes before. He can tell us all about it." Joe turned to his father. "Is the hurricane going to come to Lake Okeechobee?"

Father took off his raincoat and rubbers. "Well, I was listening to the radio over at Hank's. The storm is headed this way and should be here around 4:00."

"Is it going to be very bad?" Dave asked.

"I don't imagine so," Father said, joining the boys at the window. "It probably won't get much worse than it is now."

"Is it safe to be on the island? Will the house be OK? I've heard that some hurricanes blow roofs off." Joe shivered at the thought.

"Yes, some hurricanes have fierce winds, but I hear that this one isn't so bad. Besides, this house is brand-new, and it would take an extra-fierce wind to do it any damage."

"Dinnertime!" Mother interrupted the discussion. "Get washed up and come to the table before everything gets cold."

"Mr. Anderson says he's going to take his family and go to the mainland," Father announced as he helped himself to some rice and beans.

"Do you think we ought to leave too?" Mother asked.

"No need to. The storm's not going to be so bad. The Andersons are the only ones I've heard of who are leaving."

As Mother did the dishes after dinner, Father looked out the kitchen window, deep in thought. He could see the waters of Lake Okeechobee beating against the shores of the island. The big pine tree in the yard swayed dangerously, and the hedge was being uprooted little by little. The wind had definitely gotten stronger since he had come home.

"You know, Grace"—Father ran his fingers through his hair—"this storm might be worse than the radio announcer predicted."

"Don't you think we ought to get to the mainland?"

"Well, not right now, anyway. We'll see how thing go. If it gets any worse, we might go just for safety's sake."

The afternoon dragged on. Joe and Dave tried to get interested in games, but the scene out the window finally claimed their undivided attention.

"It's definitely gotten worse out there!" Joe exclaimed.

"I've never seen anything like it," Dave said for the third time.

"Joe, Dave, you had better get your coats," Mother finally said. "Your father and I have decided to go to the mainland. The water is rising, and we're afraid the bridge may be washed out. He's outside starting the car."

Just then Father walked back into the house. "We'll never be able to take the car," he said. "The water is above my knees. We'll have to use the boat."

He led the family to the boat, which was tossing about. They all piled in.

"What's the matter with this crazy motor?" Father said after giving the cord another yank. "I guess it's dead again. I'm going to have to take it downtown to get it fixed."

"What will we do now?" Mother sounded worried. "We can't stay here. There's no telling how high this water will rise."

"You're right. I'm beginning to think that myself." Father pulled his collar close to his neck. "It's uncommonly cold for this time of year. We had better get into town as quickly as we can."

"Maybe we should start walking," Mother suggested. "It isn't far."

As Joe stepped out of the boat, the flow of the water almost knocked him down. Grabbing hold of the boat, he regained his balance and began to follow the others.

His legs soon got tired. Walking against the

strong current was like trying to walk through a wall. The wind and rain weren't helping either. The rain was beating on the back of his head and neck, and the wind brought tears to his eyes.

"Mom, I can't go any farther." Joe felt more tired than he had ever felt in his life. And it seemed that he was getting nowhere in the turbulent waters. For every step he took, he seemed to be washed back two.

"Please, dear, try to keep moving along." Mother gave him her hand for reassurance and assistance. "The Parkers' packing house is just ahead, and we can stop there."

The McDonalds weren't the only ones who had decided to find shelter in the Parker building. There were 18 others inside.

"Well, if it isn't the McDonalds!" someone said.

"Thought y'all were going to sit this one out."

"It isn't the driest or warmest place, but come on in and join the group."

Such greetings welcomed them as the McDonalds found themselves among neighbors and friends.

The water was already waist-deep in the building, so the weary family joined the rest of the group sitting on truck cabs. Everyone tried to make the conversation light—as light as people can force a conversation to be under such circumstances.

The rising water soon forced them to the top of the trucks. The conversation weakened and finally died. Everyone was left to their own thoughts.

The building was made of wood and was not very sturdy. To those inside, it seemed as if the surging waters would surely collapse it any minute. It was swaying and straining with each swell of water, like a wild animal trying to get free of its leash.

As the rising water forced people to seek refuge in the rafters, the silence deepened. Even at this high place, they soon found their feet dangling in water.

Joe's thoughts were in turmoil. Was this the end? He was afraid to die. He blinked back the tears, afraid that someone might see him. But then he realized how ridiculous that was. He couldn't even see his hand in front of his face. It was only 5:00 and already pitch-dark. A lump welled in his throat as he felt the water slowly creep up his chest. What was he going to do? The roof was right above his head. He couldn't even get his fist between it and his head. The water was surely going to rise up and drown him.

With every movement of the swaying building, Joe felt his heart jump up into his throat. "Mom!" he cried. He couldn't see her, but he knew that she was there beside him. "What's going to happen to us?" He couldn't disguise the fear and panic in his voice.

"Say a little prayer, Joe. God will help us." The touch of her hand covering his felt warm, even in the icy water.

Sitting on the rafter, Joe could feel the building

rise and settle with each swell of the water. He could feel the water swirling all around him. It was muddy and cold and up under his chin now. A few more inches, and it would cover him completely.

Then suddenly the water snatched him off his perch, and he felt himself swirling about. He kept going down, down, and still farther down. He couldn't hold his breath any longer. Then he felt a strong hand grab him and pull him up. He found himself lying on the roof with his father beside him. Father was pulling others up through a hole in the roof.

What on earth was happening? He discovered that the dike had broken and sent still more water rushing to destroy everything in its pathway. Nothing could stand before it. The building had been torn up, but the roof was floating.

As a stump came by, Joe's father grabbed hold of it, put Joe between him and it, and hung on for dear life. The wind was making so much noise that the two could not have talked had they wanted to, and the stump kept rolling so that half the time they were underwater.

Joe was more frightened than he had ever been in his whole life. Then he remembered what his mother had said about prayer. Where was Mother? Was she all right? And Dave—were they both safe? He couldn't know. He could only pray. "Dear Jesus, please save us," he breathed fervently. It was only a simple prayer, but he felt safer, as if Jesus were there and would take care of them all.

After floating about a mile and a half, they came near enough to a pumping station to be helped in, and there Joe and his father stayed the remainder of the night. Sleep would not come easily for them, though. They were fearful that the rest of the family had perished. Finally, just before dawn, sheer exhaustion closed their eyes and minds to the horrors of the night.

Morning brought the joyful news that Dave and Mother were safe, and a few hours later the whole family was together again. "Oh, Mom!" Joe cried, running into her arms. "We were afraid that you and Dave were dead."

She hugged him tightly. "This seems too good to be true," she sobbed. "Thank God that we're alive and safe."

No one was ashamed of tears now, for they were tears of joy.

Father asked Mother, "Where did you spend the night?"

"On a telephone pole," she said.

"On a telephone pole?"

"When the building collapsed, I caught a piece of it and floated on it until I came to a telephone pole. I decided that it would be safer to stay there than to float any farther. So I tore my dress and used it to tie myself to the pole."

"But weren't you scared?" Joe asked.

"Yes, dear, I think everyone was more than a little scared last night."

Joe looked at his brother. "Where were you, Dave? On a telephone pole too?"

"No, I spent the night on a piece of the roof from the building we were in."

"You spent the whole night on a piece of the roof?" Father couldn't believe it.

"Yep." Dave threw his shoulders back a little. "The men who brought me back said that I floated four and a half miles."

"Where to?"

"Out into the Everglades," he answered.

"Boy, I bet you were really scared!" Joe said.

"No, I wasn't too scared." Dave's shoulders went back a little farther yet. "In fact, I even went to sleep."

They all laughed. It was so good to be together again. They hadn't been apart for long, but they had feared it would be forever. Now they were safe. They could go home.

Home? Was home still there? The thought hadn't crossed anyone's mind until now.

After the water had receded, they made their way back to the island, but the going was difficult.

Dragging through the mud and slush, they surveyed the destruction all around. Fear tore at their hearts as they began to picture how things would probably look.

When they reached their place, a cry escaped Mother's lips. "Our home! Our beautiful, brand-new home. It isn't here!"

Their excitement vanished as they walked over to the desolate lot where their house had been.

"Look!" Father stooped down to get a close view. "You can see where it was torn from the foundations."

"There's not a board left." Joe's eyes swept the place where his home had stood.

"You can hardly tell that a house was ever here!" Dave kicked around in the mud. Then his foot hit something solid. "Hey, what's this?" He dug down in the thick mud and pulled up something. Scraping it off, he yelled, "Look—one of our spoons!"

"I wonder how it stayed here when nothing else did." Mother took it from him. She couldn't help thinking of the other pieces of the set that were now missing.

"What's this?" Joe was pulling at something else. "Your glass pitcher, Mom!" He handed it to her, muddy but whole.

She couldn't keep back the tears. She remembered the piano the pitcher had been on when she last saw it and the beautiful gladiolus that had been in it. "This is all we have left in the world—a spoon and a pitcher! What are we going to do now?" She looked at each of them.

"Mom," Joe put his arms around her waist, "we still have one another."

Yes, they still had one another. The storm had claimed more than 2,000 lives, yet here they stood together, unharmed and strong—an unbroken family.

They looked at one another and smiled through misty eyes. They had so much to be thankful for.

4

The Drop That Saved

by Yvonne R. Bullock

O n sunny Sabbath afternoons Gordon and his dad liked to go for a walk or drive around the Napa Valley in California. This particular Sabbath was no exception. So after dinner they got into the Model T and jogged off down the road.

"Where shall we go this time?" Dad asked.

"Oh, let's go to the old quicksilver mine across the valley," Gordon answered as he took from his pocket a candle and a few matches.

"Now, how did you know that you were going to need those?" Dad teased.

Gordon just grinned.

Soon they were at the old mine. They parked the car and walked up to the mouth. Gordon lighted the candle and then put the rest of the matches back in his pocket.

He took the lead, and his dad followed behind, looking over Gordon's shoulders. They were interested in the quartz—the dark-red streaks that contained the ore from which mercury is melted. They walked slowly, inspecting the sides of the tunnel, and Dad reminded Gordon of how the flood must have had a part in depositing these minerals so deep down in the earth.

Water seeped through the rocks, dripping off the ceiling and trickling down the sides of the tunnel. The candle in Gordon's right hand burned brightly, casting long shadows behind them. The light shone in their eyes, making the floor immediately in front difficult to see. They groped their way along, their attention fixed on the rocks at their sides.

Suddenly a drop of water fell from the ceiling onto the candle. The flame went out instantly, and Gordon and his dad froze in their steps.

They began feeling the rocks on the sides of the tunnel, searching for a dry place on which to strike a match. Finally the underside of a rock that jutted out from the wall provided a spot.

Gordon pulled a match from his pocket and struck it. Its small flame lasted for only a moment, but from its light Gordon saw in front of him. There was a big, dark hole in the floor where a shaft used to be! He jumped back, bumping into his dad.

"L-l-look!" he stammered, pointing to the hole.

But just then his match went out, so his dad didn't have a chance to see. They quickly lighted the candle, and then Gordon's dad saw the hole. It was an abandoned vertical shaft, reaching down to a lower level of the mine to provide air circulation.

Gordon's dad gasped and then exclaimed, "Why, that hole could be 100 feet deep! If we had kept going . . ." But he didn't finish the sentence, thinking of the awful consequences.

He picked up a rock and dropped in into the hole. The two waited, holding their breath, as they listened carefully for the rock to hit the bottom. All was silent, and then finally—*thud! Boom, boom, boom!* It echoed and reechoed through the various levels of the mine's tunnels.

"Let's go back now," Dad said as he took Gordon's hand.

The two turned and started back.

As they were climbing into the Model T, Dad said, "If we had taken another step or two as we were looking at the rocks in the wall of the tunnel, we could have both been killed. I believe it was our guardian angel that made our candle go out just at that very instant! Let's thank our heavenly Father right now for sparing our lives."

And I've also thanked God many times. Because if they had fallen down that hole, I would never have been born. You see, Gordon is my father.

5

No Way Through

by Mary L. Anderson

L es Anderson bounded down the dormitory hall, clipped around the corner to the telephone booth, impatiently dialed a number, and waited. "Hi, Lloyd. I was wondering—do you have any time this afternoon to take a dive in Pine Lake? We need to log a few more hours for our scuba diving class."

Lloyd agreed to meet Les at 12:30. Les returned to his room and assembled his gear like a student frantically trying to finish an assignment five minutes before class. "Fins, tank, regulator, wet suit, snorkel—I guess that's all," he mumbled. "I wonder about the knife. Maybe I should take it along like I'm supposed to, just in case something happens."

He was slightly amused at the idea of needing a knife in Pine Lake—a shallow lake in Alberta, Canada—but he heaved the knife into his suitcase. It landed with a clatter close to the snorkel. Even though Les's diving made his dad uneasy, Les argued, "It's just as safe as driving a car—if you know the rules."

Soon Les and Lloyd Kuhn were driving to the end of a rutty road. As they stepped out of the stuffy car, they noticed a huge sheet of ice in the middle of the lake. It was the Friday before Easter, so it had not had a chance to melt. But they weren't concerned. There was plenty of room to dive along the shore. The boys pulled on their wet suits. Even with the sun shining, it was chilly enough to send the crows back south.

"Wow! That's cold," Lloyd gasped when he first felt the water. "Extremely cold, as a matter of fact."

"Worse than taking an ice-cold shower first thing in the morning." Les shivered.

The boys walked into the lake slowly, trying to reduce the first shock of cold water as it seeped into their wet suits. But after their bodies had warmed the water inside the rubber suits, they felt reasonably comfortable.

They stayed close together, rigorously applying the buddy system by each holding tightly to the end of a stout rope. They followed each other like a little brother tagging behind his big brother. They could see only two feet ahead in the murky water. So they knew that if they separated and one ran into trouble, the other would never be able to find his buddy in time to give any help.

After some time, they surfaced. "Shall we quit, or go out again?" Lloyd sputtered, trying to get the water out of his mouth.

"Just one more dive!" Les answered enthusiastically. "This time let's follow the bottom down and see what we can find in that slimy mud."

Submerging once again, they followed the downward slope of the lake. It got darker and colder as the depth increased. With 30 minutes of air used, Les motioned to go to the top. Up, up, up they went, sensing everything getting lighter and warmer. Or was it? Were they imagining it? It was not warmer. It was not lighter!

To their horror, they found the large sheet of ice floating calmly and defiantly right above them! With mocking coldness, it separated them from air and safety.

We're trapped under solid ice . . . No hope . . . No way out . . . Almost no air . . . If only we could see beyond these two feet. If only my cumbersome equipment wouldn't get in the way. If only . . .

Les's thoughts were as confused as a tangle of telephone wires after a hurricane. *Where are we? How far under the ice have we come? How long will my air last? Which way is the shore? Is it all over? Is this to be our last dive? It must be the end—the end. Oh, no, God. Don't let it be the end. Help us. Help us get out. Make the air last. Please.*

They were in a difficult situation, desperate and confusing. They couldn't talk any better underwater than they could with their mouths stuffed with cotton. The only way they could "talk" to each other was by making motions with their arms.

Knife. Use the knife. The thought broke through Les's foggy brain like sunlight through storm clouds. Of course—his knife. He felt for the handle strapped to his leg. There it was. *Tight, now! Don't drop it! Chip the ice!*

"It's so hard, God. Takes so long to chip. Help us make it. Help us go fast enough—don't let this be the end." He chipped furiously, as hard and as fast as his bulky gear would allow. But the ice was harder than steel.

Even with Lloyd alternating with him, Les was beginning to feel as if he had been struggling all day to get away from sharks. Les measured the depth of the ice with his hand. Yes, they were making some progress. But the ice was eight inches thick—eight inches that seemed like eight tedious feet.

"Just a little longer. Just give us a few more minutes," he breathed silently to his heavenly Father. "A few more minutes."

Then as Les made one last energetic thrust of the knife, the ice splintered and spilled over the jagged edges of the escape hatch. Les looked at his air indicator. Two minutes of air left. "Thank You, God," he whispered.

6

Caught in the Oven

by Bernadette Rajotte

You silly, silly creature! Get out of that oven immediately!" Impatiently I scolded Mr. Simms, our old tomcat. He always insisted on sleeping in the lukewarm oven.

"Someday that cat is going to be roasted alive," I declared to Mama.

But what nearly happened to our old tomcat nearly happened to my brother, Lou, and me. And we were supposed to have "more sense," as Mama put it.

It happened one rainy morning. Hetty, my best friend, was sick in bed with measles, her house was quarantined, and I was forbidden to go near for at least three weeks.

I didn't like rainy days because there wasn't anything to do. I had two older sisters who helped Mama do the housework. So all that was left for me to do was tidy up my room and help with the dishes. That didn't take long.

After a discouraging attempt to amuse myself by playing storekeeper with Lou, I gave up and sat dejectedly at the window watching the raindrops fall.

"Are you still moping about the rainy weather, Bonnie?" Mama asked as she came into the room. "Well, the rain's letting up, and I need bread and cookies from the bakery. Here's the list and the money. Take Lou with you, and don't forget your umbrellas."

Lou and I were delighted. It was always fascinating to go to the bakery and watch the giant mixers turning mounds of fresh, sweet-smelling dough. And we liked to see Mr. Hudson, the baker, in his white apron and cap, cutting, molding, and patting big lumps of dough into shiny bread pans.

But we especially got excited when the bread was done and the baker opened the giant ovens. With the use of long-handled paddles he would take out the golden loaves that crackled with warmth. The delicious smells always made my stomach hunger for a thick slice right then and there.

In no time at all Lou and I arrived at the bakery shop. We walked in and set down our umbrellas to drip. But the shop was deserted. Then I remembered that it was the noon hour.

"What will we do now?" I said. "Mr. Hudson's

probably having dinner in his house next door."

"Let's look around," Lou said. "We can go see the cool oven while we wait for the baker to return."

"What's a cool oven?" I asked.

"The baker has three ovens," Lou explained. "Two are for baking bread and cookies. The other one's fancier. It has a tile floor, and it's used for baking soda crackers. Mr. Hudson doesn't use it very often, only when he gets a special order. That's why it's called a cool oven. It's shut off from the furnaces below by big sheet iron dampers."

I didn't understand everything Lou said, but I was curious. Mama declared that I was too curious for my own good and that someday—unless I used good sense—I would find myself in great difficulty.

Without thinking, I raised the latch of the heavy iron door and peered into the cool oven. "Why, it's just like a cave, isn't it, Lou?"

"Let's crawl in and pretend we're pirates or hibernating bears," suggested Lou.

"That's a good idea!" I climbed after him into the gloomy interior of the cool oven.

We sat in silence for a few minutes. Then suddenly the iron door closed behind us with a resounding clang. Only a sliver of light shone inside between the doorjamb.

"Oh, Lou!" I cried. "We're locked in! We'll suffocate! We'll die!"

"No, we won't," he said. "All we have to do is shout. The baker will let us out."

Lou yelled for Mr. Hudson. He kicked the oven door, but to no avail. The baker had started the other two ovens, and the noise of the machinery drowned out our frantic cries. Unless we were rescued soon, the air in our cave was bound to become stale. Already our throats felt dry and hoarse from yelling. And because of his height, Lou was forced to stay in a half-bent position that strained his back. Again and again we shouted and pounded on the oven door, but no one came to let us out.

I began to sob, and Lou put his arm around me. "Don't cry, Bonnie. Perhaps the baker will hear me this time."

Lou yelled and kicked all over again. But no one answered.

Suddenly we were startled by a scraping noise, as though a damper was being opened beneath us. A breath of hot air fanned our cheeks. If I had been afraid of suffocating, I was now doubly afraid—of being roasted alive.

"Oh, no!" I cried. "Mr. Hudson is heating the oven! We're really going to die now!" I was terrified. "Now we're worse off than our old tomcat ever was!" The grim joke helped make us feel a bit better.

"Don't give up hope yet," Lou said. "We've only been in here a few minutes. Perhaps heating the cool oven was just a mistake and the baker will close the dampers."

But the tile floor of the oven was getting hot to the touch. Fortunately, Mama had made us wear our heavy shoes that rainy day. We crouched on our heels or stood up as best we could, not daring to touch the hot walls or roof with our hands and heads.

The air was getting quite stifling now, and my hair became damp and clung to my sweaty cheeks. *Poor Mama. We'll never see her again,* I thought.

"Oh, Lou," I said aloud, "let's pray for help! God always hears the prayers of children. Mama said so."

While we said a short, frantic prayer, I dug both fists into my apron pockets. My right hand touched Mama's bakery list, and right then I thought of an idea. "Lou, do you still have the pencil and string that you used when we were playing storekeeper this morning?"

"Yes," he said. He fished them out of his pocket. "But what are you going—"

"Quick, then," I said. "Punch a hole in this paper with the pencil, and tie the string through. Do you have a match?"

Just how he happened to have one I don't know, because we were never allowed to play with matches. But he had one.

"Give it to me," I said. "When I strike it, write HELP on the back of this shopping list."

I struck the match, and in the flickering light Lou wrote. The match went out, and we were in darkness again.

Lou asked, "What are you going to do with all this?"

"The door," I answered faintly. "Dangle the piece of paper up and down in the crack between the door and the doorjamb."

Painfully Lou knelt at the oven door and slid the paper through the crack. Holding the string, he pulled the paper up and down to attract the attention of the baker. But nothing happened.

Lou kept jerking the paper up and down, up and down. Once I heard him suck in his breath, and I knew that it was because of the searing pain in his knees. After what seemed ages to us but was probably only seconds, we heard a muffled yell.

The latch was lifted, the door flew open, and we fell into the arms of the terrified old baker. I felt my lungs slowly filling with pure fresh air. Dr. Harrison was called, and in a few minutes he was applying mentholated bandages to our burned hands and knees.

"I received an order for soda crackers. That's why I heated the cool oven," the baker explained to Dr. Harrison. "How was I to know that these children were hiding inside my oven?" The poor man! He was really very patient with us considering how silly we had been.

The doctor took us home, and Mama nearly fainted at the sight of our bandaged hands and knees.

"Your children are fine," the doctor explained, "just fine, except they won't be playing ball for a while." He handed her two loaves of bread and a dozen sugar cookies. "These are a gift from the baker."

It was weeks before I was able to see my best friend, Hetty. Dr. Harrison had told her all about what had happened. When finally we did get to see each other, she scolded me soundly. "What made you do such a silly thing?" she said. "Oh, I know. It was your curiosity. I do suspect that you've no more sense, after all, than Mr. Simms, your tomcat. But I'm glad you didn't turn into a burnt soda cracker!"

"And I'm glad you're over the measles at last," I said.

We both laughed. But I have often wondered what would have happened if I hadn't thought about using the shopping list and Lou's string. And I have never forgotten that the idea came to me while Lou and I were praying.

Flight to Freedom

by Jim Saunders

The fearful drone of a plane broke through the war-torn sky over occupied France during World War II. Madame Bertin looked up through the window of her small stone cottage and shuddered. "There goes another one," she said to her husband, Henri. "It is probably on a bombing raid against our allies." Her eyes grew sad as she thought of the many sorrows that had come to her country. "These are sad times we live in," she murmured as she turned from the window.

Above her in a small space between a beam and the thatch, two young men also listened to the drone of the place. Jean-Paul and Andre were Seventh-day Adventist students who had been attending the Sorbonne University in Paris when war broke over Europe. They had joined the French underground and had been successful in helping many Jewish refugees escape into Spain and Switzerland. Soon, however, the German secret police, called the gestapo, had caught up with them, and they had been thrown into prison. Several months had gone by before they had made an escape, and now they too had become refugees in the underground.

The underground had sheltered them for several weeks and had moved them across the dangerous French countryside from Paris to Annemasse, near the Swiss border. Now they were hidden in the home of Henri and Gabrielle Bertin, who were also Adventists, in the village of Meillerie on the shore of Lake Leman. Unknown to her neighbors, Madame Bertin was also a busy member of the underground and had helped many people to cross the lake into free Switzerland. She and her husband had received Jean-Paul and Andre with open arms and with fear, for the German gestapo were watching the towns along the shore very closely. The gestapo had searched the cottage several times, and each time the boys had huddled silently against the thatch while Madame Bertin prayed earnestly that they wouldn't be found.

"All is clear," whispered Madame Bertin. "There are no gestapo around now, so you can come down and have something to eat. One of our church members will come for you tonight when it is dark to take you across the lake."

The boys came down into the cheerful room that was kitchen, dining room, and sitting room for the Bertins. As they ate, Madame Bertin packed a few clothes and some food for them.

The sun finally sank down in a blaze of golden glory. Madame Bertin thanked God that there was still some beauty in her sad world. For a few minutes the sky glowed softly like a rosy ember and brought her a sense of peace. Although her country was under enemy occupation, Madame Bertin knew that God was still in supreme command.

Soon there came a knock at the door. The boys pulled their heads back into their hiding place, and Madame Bertin opened the door. A stout farmer entered.

"All is in readiness, Madame," he whispered. "We must go with great caution, for the gestapo are everywhere tonight. A large party of Jews escaped to Montreux two days ago, and they swear that not another shall pass them."

He looked up into the corner of the roof where the boys were listening. "Are you willing to take the risk?" he questioned.

"*Oui, monsieur*," came the quick reply.

The boys came down, and Madame Bertin hurried to gather up the bundle she had prepared for them. As they stepped out of the door, she thrust a small book into Jean-Paul's trembling hand. It was a little Bible. "God go with you," she whispered.

The farmer and the two boys fled like hurried shadows, being careful to keep undercover whenever possible. Several times they had to hug the ground when a patrol passed. The farmer led them through the woods that bordered the village and down to the water's edge.

"This is as far as I can take you," he explained. "When you are halfway across the lake, you will be in Switzerland. Go in haste, for the Germans patrol the shore every half hour. They should have passed this spot 10 minutes ago."

Jean-Paul followed Andre into the boat, and the farmer gave it a push out into the lake.

Silently and swiftly the boys rowed across the still waters of the lake. The night seemed hushed and quiet but full of sinister eyes. *"Go in haste; go in haste!"* The words of the farmer passed through their minds like a chant. Suddenly they heard the noise of a motor, and a searching beam of light fell across the prow of their boat.

"Jean-Paul," gasped Andre. "It's the gestapo!"

"Achtung!" boomed a German voice from the patrol boat. "Stop before we shoot!" The police boat was still far off, but the voice coming through a loud-speaker was loud and clear.

"Dear God," prayed Andre, "don't let the gestapo capture us. Please help us to escape."

Jean-Paul prayed too. And as he prayed he became aware of something pressing against his chest under his coat. It was the Bible Madame Bertin had given him. The blessed book reminded him of his favorite text, and even in deep fear he repeated to himself, "The angel of the Lord encampeth round about them that fear him, and delivereth them" (Psalm 34:7, KJV).

As he repeated the verse, the moonlight began to fade. What was happening? He looked at Andre and saw that a thick fog was settling down over the lake. The German patrol boat had already faded from view.

Quickly the boys rowed their boat off at an angle, and none too soon. The gestapo boat quickly approached them, cutting the motor as it came. A sharp staccato sound broke though the milky fog, and a spray of bullets peppered the little rowboat. The boys quickly threw themselves to the floor as another wave of gunfire passed over them. Miraculously, they weren't touched. Then a deep silence followed.

"Where are they?" Jean-Paul's hoarse whisper broke the thick silence.

Andre peered into the blinding fog. "I don't know. I can't see or hear a thing." He was interrupted by the sudden whir of motors going out into the lake. The patrol boat circled a few times and then headed back toward the French shore.

As the sound died away, the boys breathed a prayer of thankfulness and began rowing for the Swiss shore again. Soon the prow of their boat ran gently aground on Switzerland's free shore. The boys were safe. They jumped out and fell to their knees in prayer, grateful to God for guarding their lives.

8

Now See!

by Brian Sayer

The sparkling carpet of freshly fallen snow dazzled me as I zigzagged down the crooked trail of Song Mountain, a majestic peak in central New York. All around me were exuberant student friends weaving in and out among one another like knitting needles, their ski trails forming crisscross patterns in the snow. Because we'd worked so hard selling subscriptions for our school paper, this whole day was ours to enjoy—a skier's holiday.

"Watch out for that icy patch!"

My reverie was broken by the sharp warning from Soni, my skiing partner. I veered sharply to avoid the treacherous, glistening sheet that blanketed the turn.

I was uneasy on ice, especially on skis. Ever since I could remember, I'd never felt really competent when ice separated me from firm ground. But Soni, tall and slim, agile as a trapeze artist, easily skirted the slippery mass, her willowy form conveying the idea that skiing was no effort at all—and for her, it wasn't. Her auburn hair flowed from side to side in the breeze as she shifted her weight on her skis.

Trying to keep up with her, I felt more like a soldier on parade with his feet bound! My legs were rigid, my balance uncertain. Anyone could tell that I was an amateur.

I drew up beside Soni. "Say, how about a race to the lodge? Bet I'll beat you this time!" I'd never beaten her yet, but presumption is a trait of mine.

Her emerald eyes sparkled with enthusiasm; her lips tightened with determination as her every muscle grew taut for this challenge. "You can try!" she teased. "Go!"

We were off on our own private contest, leaving the main group behind. Being on the inside, I gained a slight lead on the first turn. Gleefully I swept past her and edged toward the center of the trail. But not for long! The swish of her skis and the thud of her poles on the icy crust told me that she was closing the gap between us.

"I'll take you on this curve!" she yelled against the wind. Her lithe body bent forward as she put action into her words.

"Not if I can help it, you won't!" I laughed, determined to show her at last.

But this "S" curve was icier than the rest. Sweeping too widely across the slick expanse, I lost control and landed on my back against a slender maple. I was a tangled mass of skis and poles! Although unhurt, I was slow at disentangling myself and regaining my balance. Chagrined, I snowplowed around the curve to where Soni waited.

"That's the third time you've wiped out on that curve! Didn't you see the sign that said TURN LEFT?" Her dancing eyes betrayed her stern mockery.

"All right, I get the point! I'll give up trying to conquer that one. Let's find a way to cut around on the next trip." I bowed low, gesturing toward the open trail. "Shall we continue our descent to the lodge?"

With a slight nod and graceful sweep of her arm, she replied, "After you!"

The lodge, a chaletlike structure with peaked roof and large windows, rested snugly at the junction of all the trails. Through several doors a constant stream of humanity flowed to and from its spacious interior.

"Let's get something hot to drink before we head up again, OK?" I suggested as we neared the lodge.

"Great idea! Oh, there's Doug and Janice! Hey, you two—want to have some hot chocolate with us before we try the next slope?"

"Sure, man! Let's go!" Doug answered for both of them.

As we sat around the roaring fireplace, I thought of

the slippery "S" curve and flinched awkwardly. "Say, Doug, is there any way to bypass that icy double curve on Moonlight Trail? Know the one I mean?"

"Yeah. It's a real bone rattler! But just before you come to it, there's a short cutoff to the left that'll take you completely around it, then back onto the trail below the second curve. Watch out, though; the detour is narrow and rough. You'll be all right if you keep to the left."

"Thanks a lot. I think we'll try it before we leave."

Late that afternoon Soni and I stood near the top again. She beamed at me with expectation. "Think we'll make it OK this time?"

"Sure; it shouldn't be half as hard if we take the detour." I hoped my confidence was evident. This time I had to do things right!

Amid a glittering spray of snow we shoved off, the afternoon breeze pungent with the odor of pine needles. I observed with slight misgivings how "sticky" the snow was becoming under the sun's direct rays, how difficult it seemed to maneuver.

All went well as we rounded the gentle curves. *One more turn*, I mused. *This time I must make good.*

As the cutoff appeared on the left, I automatically shifted weight for the turn. "This is it!" I flung over my shoulders. "Here goes!"

In a blinding flash, though, I was thrown into an icy bank. As I thudded to a stop, something razor-sharp grazed my right eyebrow and buried itself in the snow. Dazed, I lay motionless in a sad heap. Then, as Soni slalomed to a halt beside me, I began groping for my skis and poles.

"What happened?" Her voice trembled slightly.

"I-I-I don't know! It all h-happened s-so fast! I was up one minute and down the next! I'm all right now, but wh-where's my other ski and pole?"

The right ski, which had snapped like a twig as I fell, lay embedded in the dense snow. Its severed head was buried a foot beneath the surface. Turning to locate the other ski pole, I sickened with terror.

"Oh," I gasped weakly. "Soni, that pole is exactly where my head was a few seconds ago! Its sharp point brushed my eyebrow so close that it could have—"

"Oh, no!" Her face mirrored the horror I felt at what might have been. "Thank God it didn't happen!"

"Yes," I replied weakly, "thank God!" My hand brushed my eyebrow where there was still an old scar near my right temple.

Finally we gathered our poles and skis (fragments of one ski, for me) and rather clumsily began the difficult trek on foot down the mountainside. While we trudged along, my thoughts flashed to an autumn day four years before, when another missile had slashed me across my eyebrow.

The scene: a baseball game with my eighth-grade

teacher at bat. A swing, a miss, a bat slung from a muscular arm. A sickening blow to my skull. Then the searing pain and blood flowing from a gash by my right eye.

Less than half an inch from tragedy—not once, but twice! I realized shakily as Soni and I slipped and slid down the snowy incline. Who could doubt that it was God's hand that had twice spared my sight—perhaps even my life?

By the time we reached the end of the trail, the sun was sinking behind Song Mountain, and evening shadows cast a ghostly aura over the nearly empty slopes. Gratefully we joined the late skiers heading for the lodge.

Entering the warm, friendly structure, I paused with fresh interest in front of an array of broken skis that adorned one wall of the room. Each ski was labeled. Each ski told a tale of falls and mishaps—some minor, some major.

I watched with a sense of ceremony as the latest addition—a broken red ski, inscribed January 22, 1969—was mounted beside the others. For this memorial I felt a very special attachment. It, no less than the scar above my eye, would always speak eloquently of God's watchcare over my life. As we walked from the lodge to our cars, I lifted my gaze to the swiftly darkening sky. "Whatever it is, Lord," I whispered, "count me in!"

Stuck!

by Isabelle Edminster

Bitter winds picked up the sandlike snow and blasted it against the frosted windowpanes. Mother Burton paced uneasily from one room to the other of the rambling farmhouse, peering anxiously out of first one tiny unfrosted area and then another.

"I do declare," she said half aloud, "I don't remember seeing such a blizzard in many a day."

Yet somewhere out in this blinding Wisconsin "wollypopper" were her husband and their three daughters. More than an hour ago Father Burton had struck out in the boxy old Buick to work his way to the school building four miles away. This was no time for the girls to be out on the road walking home.

He had warmed up the "old buggy" with a tin of coals under the oil pan for a half hour. When he had pressed the starter, the engine had come to life with a good, steady hum, seemingly eager to take on the defiant drifts.

Pressing his foot on the accelerator, Father had gradually gained a little momentum. Faster and faster the Buick had plowed its way along, the snow churning out from beneath its wheels. Losing just about all his speed by the time a drift was surmounted, Father would once more drive down the gas pedal and surge ahead. One by one the drifts were conquered until finally he reached the main road, where the going was considerably easier.

Entering the school building just at dismissal time, Father urged his daughters to hurry. They followed him out the door. Bitter wind whipped the breath from their nostrils and sent stinging snow into their faces.

Once inside the roomy car, all seemed well. They could picture Mother back home praying for their safe return. And Father—well, everyone always said that if Mr. Burton couldn't make it through one of these wild Wisconsin blizzards, no one could.

Back home Mother was indeed asking God for the safe return of her family. Again and again she told Him of the great importance of their not getting stuck: "No telling what would happen if they'd get stuck in one of those hard snowdrifts and couldn't get out. Please, God, don't let them get stuck."

But it was getting dark, and still there was no

sound of the old car making its entrance in the drive-way. No girls stomping their snowy boots. From window to window Mother kept watch with one prayer in her heart: "Don't let them get stuck!"

The few minutes that it had taken the girls to get into the car and for the old Buick to get back onto the road brought a big difference in driving conditions. With lines of concern on his face, Father firmly grasped the wheel. Picking his way from one side of the road to the other, he found places still shallow enough to get through. With its large wheels and high-set body, the car kept plowing along.

But if the main road was this much of a challenge, what would it be like on that mile and a half of side road scarcely passable a few minutes ago? There was only one thing to do—hit those drifts, and hit them hard. So hard that there would still be a little momentum after the car got through them.

Everyone was tense as the side road came into view. The three girls sat on the edge of their seats and tried to see what was up ahead. Even with a clear windshield, there was no seeing for more than a few feet beyond the radiator. The snow in its wild drifting made everything look the same.

"It's now or never," Father muttered as he gripped the steering wheel tighter with his mittened hands.

Momentarily catching glimpses of the telephone poles beside the road helped him guess where the road should be. Down went the accelerator! Obediently the wheels went faster and faster, snow flying in every direction. Excitement and concern grew. They hit one drift with such force that they practically came to a halt before reaching the other side. Over and over the drifts were hit, slowing down the valiant old car but never quite leaving them standing.

Now, just a few yards ahead, was the stretch of road that Father knew would be the very worst. If he could just make it through that! It would most certainly require even more speed, so he drove the gas pedal to the floor. With a thud they hit the drifted mass and came to a dead standstill!

"Dead, dead as a doornail!" shouted Father above the whining wind.

Opening the car door, he slid out into the storm. He would scout ahead of them a few yards to see if shoveling might be of any help. But it was all one mountainous drift.

He waded ahead of the car a few feet, then suddenly stood motionless. There, half buried in a drift, was a logging truck right where he would have driven at full speed if the car had not stopped. Its load of logs was pointed straight toward their windshield at a dead level with the heads of his three daughters. No flare, no warning of any kind!

If the car had not gotten completely stuck, it

would have no doubt crumpled under the end of the logging truck! The thought made Father shudder from more than the cold. It took a long minute before he could rationally size up the situation before him.

Somehow he knew that if they'd been spared such a tragedy as this, they would make it home in spite of all the wind, subzero temperature, and blinding snow. They'd make it back to where Mother was waiting for them.

It was dark when the back door of the farmhouse opened with a bang to let in four cold, exhausted, hungry people.

"I do declare," Mother exclaimed in happy excitement, "this storm set up such a racket that I didn't even hear the car."

"Guess what!" burst out the youngest daughter. "Guess what! God helped us get stuck!"

10

Morning Prayer

by Marion J. Prescott

They reasoned it out. They talked about it again and again. And of course, Mother was right. She was always right. But it wasn't fair! Elsie had wanted that job. Sure, it wouldn't pay as much as the job Mother could get, but Elsie needed it to prove to herself that she could do something besides babysit and wash dishes.

And working in Dr. Heiskel's office would have been fun. The job would have taken Elsie away from the dreary sameness of a home routine. She would have met new and interesting people, and it would have given her experience for a better job next summer when she could begin saving for college.

"Oh, yes," she would have been able to say, "I worked all last summer for Dr. Heiskel getting his files in order. Typing? Answering telephones? Yes, I have had experience." And besides, Dr. Heiskel had asked her to work for him!

But it was already decided. She'd stay home and watch Robbie—big deal! And Mother would go back to work for the summer. "I've prayerfully thought it through, Elsie," Mother had said. "We need the money. You'll want nice clothes for school, and the boys will need winter coats, and the car needs repairs."

"But Marge could take Robbie. She watches her cousin Patty anyway, and Robbie would enjoy it. She could even come over—"

"I couldn't depend on anyone else the way I could you," Mother had said. "I'd worry about Robbie getting into the street. It's such a busy corner, and since they've widened the street, there are all those trucks roaring by."

There it was! Stuck all summer with a little brother. At least her other two brothers were away at camp.

One morning early in the summer Robbie was in his high chair happily playing with his cereal, and Elsie was picking up in the living room. Father had left his slippers by the chair. Yesterday's papers lay beside them. She fluffed pillows and dusted. Paula was coming by later. They were going to walk down to Robinsons. At least that would get her out of the house for a while.

Suddenly Robbie's spoon flew out of his hand, and the cereal dumped over onto the floor.

"Oh, Robbie! Now look what you've done!" she scolded.

Robbie's brown eyes brimmed with tears and then spilled over as he began to sob.

"I'm sorry, baby," she said as she cleaned up, but irritation was still in her voice.

At first it had been fun having a baby in the house, but now he was a constant problem. His fingers were into everything. She was always being stuck watching him, and now it would be for all summer long! She gave him a cracker to quiet him and a clean spoon to play with. Her feelings were mixed up and all wrong. She didn't want to resent a baby. But how could she help it?

He pounded his spoon on the chair.

"Oh, Robbie, quit it."

He did it again, and she took him out of his chair and set him in the hall with some toys while she made the beds. In her own room she slipped to her knees and prayed. "Oh, God, help me. Guide me. Be with me. Let me accept it and not resent Robbie. I love him. But I did want that job so badly. I wanted it. I wanted it," she said close to tears. "But Your will be done. Guide us and protect all of us this day. Amen."

She stayed on her knees for a long time. The telephone rang, and she got to her feet to answer it, wading through Robbie's toys.

"Oh, hi, Marge," she said. "Oh, nothing. Just watching Robbie and making beds. Why don't you come over? Pick up Paula on the way. We're going to Robinsons."

Suddenly her mind was made up. Tonight she was going to tell Mother how she felt. It was the only way to do it. Being upset with Robbie all the time wasn't good for either of them. Marge could watch Robbie as well as she could. She hung up the phone and came back down the hall. She felt better for her decision. She made the beds and went into the nursery. Robbie was playing with blocks and chattering to himself.

This is a funny little room, she thought. Her father had built the room out of a storage area when Robbie was born. It was a long, narrow room facing the street, with only one low window.

As she studied the room, she suddenly had an urge to move the furniture, to change things around. For two years now it had been just like this. *Maybe I could move the crib over to here*, she thought. *The chest of drawers could go there, and . . . No, the playpen there.*

Once again the telephone rang. "Oh, Paula," she said, "maybe I won't go after all. You and Marge go. I'm moving the furniture around in the nursery. No," she laughed, "it isn't that important. I just decided I would."

She paused. "Come over on your way back, OK? And bring Marge. I have something to ask her."

She hung up. Now, why had she done that? She had wanted to go. It was going to be a lot of work moving the furniture, and it was getting hotter by the minute. Oh, well, she'd talk to Marge about Robbie today. Mother could be persuaded.

She went back into the nursery, and for the next 20 minutes struggled and shoved the room's furniture into place. "This chest of drawers must weigh a ton," she told Robbie. He had come to the doorway to watch.

"See—see."

"Yes, Elsie's moving the furniture, Robbie, and breaking her back." For some reason that made him laugh, and she laughed with him. But as she stood looking at the room, it seemed all wrong. It was the kind of room you couldn't really change.

Just then she heard the girls coming. Marge had her cousin Patty with her. "Put her in Robbie's room," Elsie told her. "She can be in the playpen. I'm putting Robbie down for a nap. Come on, I'll show you the room."

They waded through the toys down the hall. They all stood in the doorway together.

"Sort of lopsided, isn't it?" Paula said.

"I knew you'd say that!" Elsie responded, and they all laughed.

"What got into you, anyway?" Marge wanted to know.

"Oh, I don't know. Just got an urge."

"Next time ignore that kind of urge, will you?"

"OK, I'll change it back; I get the hint." Elsie laughed. "But right now I'm just too tired. Let's have some lemonade." For the next half hour they watched TV and talked. "How about another glass, girls?" Elsie said.

"Just half," Marge responded.

Just as she held out her glass, a loud jarring crash sent it flying from her hand. There was a piercing screech of brakes. A sickening jolt shook the house as if it were being torn from its foundations. Then, after a split-second silence, both babies began screaming. The three girls ran to Robbie's room.

Elsie's knees buckled, and she fell to the floor. The front end of a diesel truck was staring at them, protruding from the long wall in the nursery!

"Elsie fainted," Marge later told her parents. "She took one look at that truck and slumped over into a dead faint, there on the floor."

"That's right where Robbie's crib was," Elsie sobbed afterward. "It has stood right there ever since he was born. It really was the only place for it. But somehow this morning"—she began to sob again—"I decided to move it.

"Oh, Mom, Dad, what if I hadn't moved it?" she

asked. "I had already promised Paula I'd go to Robinsons with her when I decided to move the furniture," she explained again, wiping her eyes and then her nose. "For no reason at all I just decided to change everything around." No matter how many times she told it, she couldn't stop marveling about it.

"How in the world could you have known?" Marge kept asking. "What came over you?"

"It was a miracle," someone said. A photographer was there from the paper.

Elsie smiled and hugged Robbie, shaking her head as she walked through the crowd. She had hardly put him down once since it happened.

"What are you thinking about, Elsie?" Paula asked her. "You have such a happy look on your face."

"I was thinking," Elsie said, "of this morning— when I prayed for guidance and protection. God heard and answered."

Midnight
in the Supermarket

by Thearon Staddon

But what should I do if someone breaks in?"

"What should you do?" Leo roared with laughter. "Why, that's why we're hiring you. Just chase them right back out again!"

I had been working part-time for nearly a year as a carryout boy at Derby Hill Market. Now my two bosses, Leo and Bill, wanted me to guard the store for several nights a week. The regular night guard, a semiretired man, had planned a vacation in Florida for six or seven weeks.

My first night on duty I tried to act brave. After all, I had turned 16 that summer. But after locking the door from the inside after hearing the good night wishes from departing employees, I lost a sizable piece of confidence.

Maybe those guns kept me as uneasy as anything. They implied more serious business than I anticipated. Bill and Leo always kept a revolver in a desk drawer and a shotgun leaning against the wall behind the office door. One of the clerks stayed to show me how to load them before he left that first night.

Besides night watching, my job included sweeping the floors, burning extra boxes, and taking out the pop bottles returned for refund. As I went about my work, I thought, *I don't know enough about guns to fool with them. If someone breaks in, I'll just flip off the lights and peg a handy can or jar in his direction. It wouldn't do him a great deal of damage, but it might frighten him away.*

After a few uneventful nights I asked Leo for permission to go to a piano concert and come in to work several hours late.

"Sure, Thearon. Just be sure you can get the sweeping done. Take the key with you, because there will be no one here when you come in."

Wind moaned through the power lines overhead, and snow hissed darkly around the store when I reached into my pocket for the key at 11:25 that night. As I let myself into the building, a glance told me that someone had forgotten to leave on the usual night-lights. I turned to relock the door behind me, but something didn't seem quite right. I felt a little better as the bolt clicked home and the whirring cooler motors and breathy-sounding furnace blower identified themselves.

As I reached for the light switch, I could hear creaks and groans throughout the store. But I reassured myself that they were just the cold biting in from outdoors. Yet there was something decidedly unsettling about the market this night. I stood for a moment with my hand on the switch, trying to pin a meaning to it all. Then from somewhere an almost soundless something was moving toward me.

"HOLD UP YOUR HANDS!" a voice boomed out.

All hope of an empty store was shattered. *So that's why the night-lights were out,* I thought.

I whirled around without putting up my hands. After all, I belonged there. By the dim glow that a streetlight cast through a frosted windowpane, I saw a man crouched behind a stack of canned goods. He held a shotgun up to his shoulder and wore a cowboy hat down over his eyes. His form looked familiar. And that cowboy hat—where had I seen one like that before?

"Bill . . . Bill . . . is that you?"

"Thearon, is that *you?*"

In a moment the lights were on and the shotgun was lying on a checkout deck. Bill and I leaned against a counter to regain our breath and let our pulses slow down.

"Why in the world are you this late, man? What happened to you? Why didn't you call someone? I came within a fraction of a twitch of shooting you! Don't you *ever* do a thing like this again!" Bill's tension almost turned to anger before he realized that I had had permission to be late.

Both Leo and I had neglected to tell the evening shift. So when no guard showed up, they called the other boss. He had come down himself to watch the store, and for the lack of a note or phone call, I came close to gaining a personal knowledge of the business end of a shotgun.

"The angel of the Lord encampeth round about them that fear him, and delivereth them" (Psalm 34:7, KJV). That text, which was a favorite of mine as a child, means more than ever to me now.

12

Terror on the Tracks

by Diana Berry Sauerwein

Hey, Di, want to take a ride?"

"Sure, Steve, only I have to be back home in an hour. I've got a lot of homework for tomorrow."

"Yeah, I know. An hour is just time for me to show you a new dirt road I found today. I'm not sure exactly where it goes. Didn't have time to follow it very far. You know how I love old roads."

Steve was familiar with just about every little back road in San Bernardino County. We climbed into the little white VW bug and headed out of town. The moon shone brightly through the trees that lined the streets.

Off to the left of San Timoteo Canyon Road we followed a dirt road as it wound its way through orange groves, becoming narrower as we went. The headlights sent two little rabbits scurrying off in the night. After a sharp turn to the left, we were on a railway service road.

Steve drove the car beside the tracks for a few hundred feet. To the right of the car were the railroad tracks, and to the left was a concrete irrigation ditch filled with about a foot of water.

Suddenly, directly in front of us, loomed a truckload of sand, completely blocking the road! There wasn't time to think. Steve tightened his grip on the steering wheel, and in a flash we were on top of the sandpile—almost! The car high-centered just a little to the right of the highest part of the pile, with the right wheels resting on the railroad tracks.

We jumped out of the car and viewed the situation. It looked hopeless, but we had to do something. Steve pulled the jack from under the spare tire in the trunk. Propping it on a railroad tie that he found close by, he began working frantically to lift the car out of the sand enough to allow us to move it forward.

When the car was as high as the jack would elevate it, Steve stopped pumping and wiped the sweat from his forehead. "You get in the car and start the engine. When I yell, put it in first gear and give 'er the gun! Don't slip the clutch!"

Steve pushed from behind while I floored the gas pedal. The car didn't budge. "Turn off the engine. I'll have to dig out more sand from under the wheels." He didn't have a shovel, but he moved as much sand as he possibly could with his hands.

"OK. Try it again!" he called.

"Here goes!" The engine roared, the wheels spun, but the car didn't move an inch.

"Think I'll let it down and use this railroad tie as a lever under the rear axle. Maybe that will work better."

Again we tried to move the car, but in vain.

"Why don't you drive it, Steve? Maybe I'm not doing it right," I suggested.

"OK. Stand on the rear bumper. Maybe the extra weight will give us more traction." Steve slipped behind the steering wheel and turned the ignition switch. The engine roared, the wheels spun, and sand sprayed out behind the car. He shifted from first gear to reverse, then back to first again. The car rocked back and forth and moved a few inches, but that was it.

Then we heard it! Low, rumbling—the sound of a train! We looked off in the distance toward the sound and saw a light moving slowly over the tops of the trees.

Fear gripped my heart with icy fingers. *What if the car is demolished by the train? What if the train is derailed, overturned? What if the passengers are injured or killed? What if we are killed?* Frantic thoughts raced around in my head.

In the moonlight Steve's face was sickly white. It seemed like ages before he spoke. "Kneel down, Di. The only thing we can do is pray."

We knelt in the sand. Steve prayed, "Dear Father, we've tried, and we can't do any more, but You can. Please help us to get loose. Thank You. Amen."

In seconds we were on our feet again. Steve ran toward the car and groped in the darkness for the jack. His foot kicked it, and it splashed into the water in the irrigation ditch. "We can't look for it now," he yelled. "Stay back. I'm going to try once more to get this thing out of here!"

"Oh, Steve, what if the train gets here before you get out of the car?"

My words were wasted. He revved up the engine. The train was in sight now, rounding a bend in the tracks. The headlight swung around and aimed straight for us. The warning whistle blew.

The car motor roared. The wheels spun, then took hold, and the car drove off the sandpile as if it had never been stuck. The train raced past and sped on down the track.

Since that night almost 10 years ago, God has answered many prayers for Steve (who later became my husband) and me—some even before they were prayed. Prayer has given us a wonderful Friend.

"And this is the confidence that we have in him, that, if we ask any thing according to his will, he heareth us: and if we know that he hear us, whatsoever we ask, we know that we have the petitions that we desired of him" (1 John 5:14, 15, KJV).

13

The Hand on the Doorknob

by Evelyn Zytkoskee

Teryl tossed on her bed. What was wrong? Why couldn't she sleep? She had worked so hard that Thursday afternoon. What freshman nursing student doesn't work hard? Her head ached, and she felt miserable. By 7:00 the next morning she realized that she would have to ask the school nurse to visit her.

"I'm sorry, Teryl," the nurse told her after taking her temperature, "but it looks like you have a touch of flu. We'd better see if the doctor wants to give you some medication."

"Can I go to classes this morning?" Teryl asked. "I've got a test in biology."

"No. I think your friends would be happy to have you keep your germs to yourself. Besides, you look like you could use some sleep."

Teryl spent the day in bed, except for a short visit

to the doctor. By evening she felt a little better and asked the dean of women whether she could stay for the weekend in the home of Mary Lou, her married cousin, who lived just off the campus. She dreaded the thought of staying in a big, empty dormitory on Sabbath morning. She received permission to go in time for Friday night supper and return to the dorm Monday morning. She promised the nurse that she would stay in bed.

Teryl tried to be sociable lying on the living room couch at her cousin's home. Several friends had been invited to supper, and they listened to sacred music as the food was being prepared. Everyone felt sorry for Teryl as they saw her flushed face and tired eyes, but she kept at a distance.

Her fever rose to 102 degrees that evening. Her cousin, a wise little mother, ushered her off to bed.

Sabbath morning Mary Lou's family was up early, scurrying around getting ready to go in various directions for Sabbath school and church. Teryl hadn't slept much. If she could only quit aching!

After everyone had gone, she decided that she would feel better if she could take a warm bath. She walked across the hall and ran the bathtub full of warm water. She had just stretched out in the tub when she heard the front door open. She thought at first that it was one of the family members who had returned for something.

She heard the heavy tread of a man's footsteps going down the hall and past the bathroom door. Then she heard dresser drawers coming out and banging shut in rapid succession. From one bedroom to the next the intruder worked with rapid thoroughness. All the hall cupboard doors clicked open and banged shut.

Teryl lay in the tub motionless with fright. Then the heavy steps came directly to the bathroom door. She offered a silent, terrified prayer for help. The doorknob turned completely around, but the door didn't open. The footsteps moved down the hall. Teryl's heart was pounding wildly. She was afraid to make a move.

Again the man returned to the unopened door and tried the knob. He tried three times, but each time the door remained closed. Just as he was turning the knob the third time, Teryl heard the telephone ring. The man heard it too and evidently became frightened, for he ran from the bathroom door. Teryl still made no attempt to move.

After a long 10 minutes of silence during which the bathwater got cooler and cooler, Teryl heard the phone ring again. This time she thought that the robber had either gone or was in the basement. She put on her nightgown and ran to the phone. "Oh, roommate," she whispered, "get some help quick. A prowler was here, and he might still be in the house. Please hurry."

Quickly she hung up and dashed out the front door and across the street to a neighbor's home. Breathlessly she told them the whole story.

The police were called but found no one. They assumed that the man had been looking for money, for he had taken nothing from the house.

"I don't remember locking the bathroom door," Teryl said again and again. "I think God told my angel to keep it shut. I'm so glad that God had His hand on that door."

14

The Limp That God Sent

by Elaine Egbert

Effie pulled her black wool cape tightly around her shoulders, picked up the satchel in which she carried her books and lunch, and let herself out of the house and into the half-light of early morning. Out of long habit she glanced toward the western sky to check the weather. Cold, crisp, clear. Just perfect for a ride.

Smiling in anticipation, she crunched through the snow toward the big red barn. There her new horse, Buff, had been brought the night before. Months earlier Uncle Grant had told her of the young stallion he was raising as a gift for her. Finally, when Uncle Grant had felt satisfied with the stallion's training both for riding and for harness, she had received a letter informing her of the date to expect his arrival by train. And so the night before, Dad had hurried to the nearby station, waited for the train, and led home her beautiful brown Buff!

As she lifted the latch and swung open the heavy barn door, a familiar nicker from Truly, her old mare, greeted her.

"Not this morning, Truly," Effie called pleasantly to the old horse. "No more long morning trudges for you! Now you can be a lady of leisure!"

The mare poked her head over the gate and rubbed it up and down against Effie's arm, as if to say, "I've carted you around ever since you were little, and I want to now." But Effie just patted her and brushed past.

A 17-year-old girl with the responsible job of teaching the county school needed a horse that could be relied on and that had plenty of energy. Effie knew that poor old Truly was nearly worn out.

Early each morning she had saddled and ridden the mare seven long miles to her one-room school-house. Then she had tied her to a limb of an old maple tree to await the time to return home. Often the students had begged for rides on Truly, and Effie had usually agreed, as the old mare loved children.

But now things were different. At last she was the owner of a spirited young horse, and she knew that she would be the envy of every other young person in the area! She would have to warn her students to stay away from Buff until she came to know his habits better.

Effie plopped her satchel down on a bale of hay,

chose a halter from the pegs on the wall, and headed toward Buff's stall at the rear of the barn. Climbing onto the gate, she held out her hand to him.

"Come on, Buff," she said softly. "Time to go to school."

Buff turned, nickered, and then cautiously approached her, his nose stretched toward her hand. Quickly Effie let herself into his stall and with soothing words slipped the halter over his head. Then, as she led him down the center aisle of the barn, she noticed that he favored his right foreleg—an obvious limp!

"Oh no!" she grumbled. "Just when I wanted to show you off!"

Disappointed, she returned Buff to his stall, patted him briefly, then headed toward Truly's stall.

"Well, old girl," she sighed, "I guess you'll have to take me today after all. Only you'll have to pull the buggy; I have too many books to carry."

Not bothering to halter Truly, she led her to the buggy, deftly harnessed her, and swung wide the barn doors. Within a few minutes she and Truly were clomping toward the schoolhouse.

It was a beautiful day, but she couldn't help feeling sorry for herself for having to wait before riding Buff. She hoped that nothing serious was wrong with his leg and made a mental note to tell Dad about it as soon as she returned home.

Effie settled back in the springy buggy and watched as they jogged through the snowy country-side. No need to worry about guiding Truly. She knew every turn.

Just before noon, while Effie taught the first-graders their reading lesson, the sky suddenly dark-ened. Surprised by the rapid change, Effie hurried to the window and looked toward the west. Fat snow clouds tumbled rapidly toward her, while overhead they had already hidden the sun.

Clinton, the oldest boy in school, rose from his desk and gazed out the window. "Miss Hawthorne, them looks like blizzard clouds. See how fast they's a-movin'?"

Just this once Effie stifled the impulse to correct Clinton's poor grammar.

"I think you'd better let school out so's the pupils kin all get home afore it hits. It looks bad!" he added worriedly.

Effie watched the clouds as they scudded angrily toward her. The school board had not mentioned anything about letting school out early in case of bad weather, but she knew that she didn't dare take a chance with the safety of the children. She hurried the smaller ones into their mittens, caps, and coats and sent them scurrying off in the care of their older brothers and sisters. She breathed a prayer that each would arrive home before the worst of the storm hit.

As Effie went about her usual chore of banking the fire in the potbellied stove that stood in the center of the schoolroom, she again thought about Buff. His young strength would have gotten her home in no time today.

After making sure everything was secure for the night, Effie slipped into her cape and mittens. She hurried down the steps and across to the maple tree where Truly patiently waited. Chilled, she harnessed Truly, catching her breath at each raw gust of wind. Effie had to laugh because it seemed that just when she would brace herself against a particularly strong gust of wind, it would stop and she would nearly fall on her face.

She climbed into the buggy and flicked the reins, and the old mare turned and headed toward home. The snow fell thickly now, and the wind drove the icy flakes, as sharp as tiny razors, into the pink of Effie's cheeks. As she watched, the wind swept the surrounding fields almost bare of snow and heaped it over the gullies and deep wheel ruts in the road. She covered her eyes with her mittened hands and peeped out between the little slits she left between her fingers, hoping to see a landmark that would tell her how far she was from home. It seemed hours since she'd left the school, though her better judgment told her that it had not been long.

The storm quickly grew to blizzard proportions.

Effie strained her eyes to see Truly, but she saw only traces of her in a blur of whiteness. As darkness settled onto the earth, Effie realized how easy it would be to become lost. She knew, too, that Truly was very cold because she moved along so slowly.

Effie's toes were beginning to lose their feeling, and the fear of freezing to death grew within her. She felt thankful for old Truly, who kept going on so bravely.

And then it happened. The buggy wheel hit a rock in the road and slid sideways into the ditch. Effie automatically tightened the reins and called encouragement to Truly, who obediently strained against the harness, but to no avail. They were stuck fast in a snowbank.

Pulling her cloak tight around her, Effie climbed down out of the buggy, keeping hold of the reins. She knew better than to let loose while she could see nothing. So she made her way, hand over hand, to where Truly stood shivering.

With numb hands she loosened Truly from the buggy, grasped her mane, and pulled herself onto the back of the faithful horse. There she clung as Truly slipped and slid forward. Once or twice Effie lifted her head to look around, but she could see nothing but snowflakes. Time and again Truly stumbled, and once she scraped Effie's leg against a fence post, but still she kept moving on.

"Dear Father, please give Truly the strength to get us home safely," Effie prayed as a warm sleepiness crept over her. She relaxed against Truly, yawned, then told herself that she must hang on to her mane tightly. The muffled thud of Truly's steps lulled Effie into a delicious half-sleep.

As she dozed, pleasant memories of her childhood returned. She had been only a little girl when Dad had bought the mare as her birthday surprise.

"Is she *truly* mine?" she had squealed, jumping up and down in glee. And that was how Truly had been named.

Suddenly Effie felt herself falling, and in her confusion she thought she was sliding off a cliff. She flailed her arms wildly in an effort to catch herself and finally felt her body resting on a firm surface. Bright lights pounded at her closed eyes, and she slowly became aware of a terrible ache all over her body. At last she roused herself enough to open her eyes. Surprised, she found that she wasn't lying at the bottom of a cliff but on her mother's bed, which was piled high with warm blankets. Mama stood on one side of the bed, rubbing Effie's hands, her face damp with tears.

Then someone entered the room and handed a cup to Mama. "Have Effie drink this warm cocoa."

Mama braced Effie's head so she could sip the warm brown liquid. And then little by little the memory of the long trek home returned to her. Alarmed, she looked across the room where Dad paced back and forth.

"Truly?" she asked, choking back a cry. "Is Truly all right?"

Dad nodded and came nearer. He took her cold hand in his big warm ones. "Yes, Effie, Truly is fine. Cold, but fine. We rubbed her down good and gave her some warm mash and a blanket. It was a good day that I bought that mare for you, for today she saved your life."

Effie lay quietly for a moment, soaking up all the warmth her body could hold. Then, remembering the disappointment she had felt that morning, her eyes clouded and she stared thoughtfully at Dad.

"And Buff? If I'd ridden him today, could he have found his way home like Truly did?"

Dad rested one booted foot on the bench at the end of the bed. "I can't say he wouldn't have, but he doesn't know this country at all. Never been over that road before. Came in on the train yesterday from a different direction."

Dad stared at the flowered wallpaper for a few moments, then straightened. "No, daughter, Buff probably wouldn't have been able to find his way back to the house."

Two fat tears slid down Effie's cheeks. To think that dear old Truly had saved her life even though she had felt cross about having to drive the old mare to school that morning!

"Dad, I didn't ride Buff this morning because of his right foreleg. He limped, so I thought I shouldn't take him."

Puzzled, Dad turned back to the bed. "Why, daughter, I rode Buff today! I wondered why you didn't take him. There's nothing wrong with his leg!"

As she came to a full realization of what a narrow escape she'd had, Effie thanked a loving God for sending a limp just when it was needed.

15

Trouble With Boastin' Is . . .

by Gar Baybrook

L et's climb Stringtown Mountain today," suggested Harvey as he and a dozen other children ate breakfast around a campfire.

"But won't we soon be hitching up the wagons to head toward Texas?" questioned his sister Myrtle. She looked around the campsite. Ten wagons were drawn up in a circle in a beautiful meadow by the side of a sparkling stream. Huge cottonwoods towered over their heads.

A little distance from the children's fire was another larger campfire. There the grown-ups gathered, laughing and talking of future plans. Their 10 families had left southeast Missouri to settle in Muleshoe, Texas. That year—1920—looked like a good year to start a new farm in the West.

But to Harvey today seemed the perfect day for a

hike right here in Oklahoma! The other boys and girls crowded around him, eager to take part.

"We're going to stay camped here for several days while the men repair harnesses and wagons," he announced. "If we start right now, we can climb clear to the top of the mountain and be back in time for dinner."

"Let's go," shouted several boys.

"Can we girls go too?" asked Myrtle, not wanting to miss the fun.

"Well, I suppose so, but you'll have to make it on your own. We're not going to spend all our time helping girls," decided Harvey.

"We can climb just as well as you," retorted Myrtle. "Come on, girls. We'll show them." And she started toward the foot of the hill.

The boys, not to be outdone, began to run, and soon they were all hurrying up the steep slopes.

"Maybe we'll see a mountain lion," said Freddy, panting.

"More likely just a jackrabbit or coyote," scoffed Harvey. "Most of the lions are farther west."

Soon they were high above the campground. They could see the white-topped wagons down among the trees. Blue smoke curled up from the campfires and hung over the cottonwoods. A hawk glided past them in sweeping circles, watching for any careless field mouse. Far below, the creek wound its way around the mountain, and they too partially circled the ridge to find an easier way up.

"Hey, look at that cave up there," exclaimed one of the boys.

"Where?" shouted several children as they scrambled up for a better view.

Soon they were all gathered around a large hole. Dirt had been dug out and piled in front, making a sort of porch. The dirt was packed down, showing frequent use.

"We better stay away," Myrtle said. "Looks as though some wild animal lives here."

"Aw, just a badger or a coyote," Harvey replied.

"I'm not so sure," Freddy said. "That's a pretty fair-sized hole."

"Well, I'm not afraid," boasted Harvey. "I'll crawl in and see what it is."

"Oh, no; don't take chances," said his sister.

But Harvey had to make good on his boast, so he dropped to his knees and began to crawl in. He decided that there was an advantage to being only 12 and skinny.

He followed the tunnel that led straight back into the hillside. The earth smelled damp and fresh, but as he crawled farther in, there was a stronger, more pungent odor. He couldn't remember that a badger smelled that way. *I'm probably smelling something a coyote dragged in here*, he thought, still not concerned.

In fact, he was rather enjoying the worried murmuring of the girls clustered around the opening.

Then the tunnel sloped up slightly, and he heard a noise. It was the sound of breathing just ahead of him! It was too dark to see, so he squeezed against the side of the tunnel and let a little daylight filter past his shoulder.

Two large green eyes stared at him unblinkingly. They weren't more than five feet ahead, and they were too big for any coyote. A low snarl sounded, and the hair on Harvey's head stood on end. He wasn't personally acquainted with any mountain lions, but he suddenly realized that he was now facing one in its lair.

He began crawling backward, keeping his eyes on those glaring green eyes. As he slowly backed out, those eyes came along too.

His hands were suddenly moist with sweat. His throat was dry, and it was hard to swallow. He wished he hadn't been so boastful. The wagon train was a long way off. None of the kids had brought a gun. Who expected such danger on a beautiful morning like this?

He gave a quick glance over his shoulder. He was still several feet from the opening. It hadn't seemed this far coming in. When he looked back toward those staring eyes, they seemed even closer!

Harvey was nearing the opening now, but with each backward step those eyes also came forward. Then he could hear the others chattering outside.

"Run for your lives!" he shouted. "There's a mountain lion following me out!"

Screams from the girls and the sound of running feet assured him that the others had believed him and had taken off down the mountain. He wished desperately that he were leading them.

After a few more backward shuffles, he was in the open. In one mad rush he straightened, turned, and leaped away from that awful cave! The slope was steep, and he was running in great bounding leaps right down the mountainside.

Behind him he could hear big soft thuds as the cat's enormous paws struck the ground. Each thud added fear and speed.

Ahead loomed a thicket of trees. It was too late to turn. He plunged among them, warding off first one trunk and then another with the palms of his hands. The rough bark tore the skin, but he was too scared to feel it.

The ground suddenly leveled out for a distance of 10 or 12 feet and dropped off into the creek 20 feet below. Harvey never slowed down, but rushed across the level spot with pounding heart. He leaped far out into the air. With legs still churning he fell with a mighty splash into the pool below.

Coming to the surface, he wasted no time swimming to the far bank. As he crawled out, dripping wet and shaking like a leaf, several of the men rushed up, their guns ready. They searched the high bank across the stream for quite a while, but no mountain lion could be seen.

"Did that mountain lion scratch you?" Harvey's father hurried to examine him.

"No, he never got quite that close." Harvey tried to control his voice. He didn't want to cry, but it was hard to hold back the tears.

"Then what's all the blood from?" his father asked.

Harvey held up his hands. Now that it was over and he was safe, he realized that his hands smarted badly. And no wonder. His palms were raw where the skin had been torn by the trees. His father led him to their wagon and wrapped both hands with cloth from a flour sack.

A careful search of the mountainside revealed large tracks of a mountain lion. But evidently the huge cat had been as frightened by the screams of the children as they had been of it. In spite of watching the cave from a nearby hiding place for a day and a night, the hunters never caught a glimpse of the lion again.

"Son, did that brush with a mountain lion teach you anything?" Harvey's father asked the next day.

Harvey thought a minute. "Yes, I guess so. I'm not going to boast anymore. The trouble with boasting is that is gets you into too much trouble too fast."

"Good," agreed his father. "Now, let's hook up the team and head on west."

16

Jagged Rocks
and a Quiet Pool

by Dale Dunston

The scorching summer sun beat down on our bare backs as a half dozen friends and I descended a steep, rocky path to the swimming hole. The hot, stony ground was almost unbearable to walk on with bare feet. As we hopped painfully down the trail, we paused occasionally in the glorious shade of some scraggly oak.

The air was heavy; not a breath of breeze stirred, and we were eager to hit the water. Finally we stood on the edge of a rock that hung out over the river. Fifteen feet below us a deep pool glistened in bright sunlight. The rugged outcropping provided an excellent diving board, and we wasted no time putting it to use.

All seven of us were in our midteens and were experienced swimmers, but none of us could match the skill Brad displayed. He was an excellent swimmer and an even better diver. He spent the whole afternoon climbing to the top of the rock, diving off, and climbing up again. His spectacular array of stunts seemed unlimited, and he never made the trip to the water in ordinary fashion.

Once he asked me whether I wanted to learn some of his tricks. I just smiled and said, "No, thank you."

"Why not?" he asked, his blue eyes dancing as the water dripped from his sandy blond hair.

"Oh, I think I'd just rather stay with swimming," I answered. "It's a lot safer."

The hours passed all too quickly, and we had to start thinking about leaving.

"Hey, before we go, let's float downstream a ways. We've never checked out those rapids," I said.

My proposal found no resistance, and soon we were all floating down the river. The current propelled us swiftly along. The river broadened and grew shallower. Brad was in the lead, and I was next. Up ahead we could hear the low rumble of the rapids as they flowed under the bridge. We had driven over the bridge many times, and the rapids hadn't looked too dangerous from its height.

When we first reached the rapids, they were merely low waves. But I lost track of Brad, and then I heard him yelling. Looking around, I finally spotted him standing knee-deep in the water along the shore. He had his hands cupped to his mouth and was shouting, "Jagged rocks! Jagged rocks! Get out—they'll kill you!"

I looked ahead. Directly under the bridge the river turned sharply to the right. It pounded fiercely against some large, jagged boulders lining the bank and churned itself into a white froth. In the middle of the channel whirlpools sucked and spun their way into the depths.

After one quick look at all this, I headed for the shore and safety. But the river had other ideas, and my best strokes fell far short of what I needed to carry me out of danger. Finding the current too strong to fight, I realized I'd have to go with it. I floated in a reclining position with my feet stretched out before me to absorb the shock in case I should hit a rock.

The speed of the river quickened, and soon I was pitched from the relative calm of the rapids into the violent holocaust I had been hoping to avoid. I tossed, spun, and rolled until I had difficulty telling which way was up. Then suddenly there were those terrible rocks, and I was being driven straight for them.

"Oh, God, save me!" I screamed the words in my mind. A different current grabbed me now and spun me away from the rocks. I shot by them, missing their cruel edges by inches.

As quickly as I had entered that watery fury, I found myself floating in a placid pool at the foot of the rapids. I had drifted into a kind of backwater off the main channel, and there was no current. I swam out into the main channel and was gently carried downstream toward the shallower water.

But then all at once I had the sensation of being grabbed by a giant vacuum cleaner. I was sucked straight down. I tried desperately to surface, but the force was so great that I could scarcely move my arms, let alone propel myself to the surface. I plunged into the green depths. I have never in my life had a greater sense of my own weakness. I was completely helpless. Once more I silently screamed, "God, help me!"

Moments later the grip of the monster relaxed, and I swam to the surface. Soon I was floundering toward the shore. At last in shallow water, I splashed and stumbled onto the warm, sandy beach. I was exhausted, and the hot sand felt good. I stretched out full-length—it was so good to be on solid ground again!

Several minutes later the rest of the guys came stumbling over the hot rocks. I had been lost from their view, and they were anxious to see whether I was all right. "What happened to you?" they asked. "Are you OK? We thought you were a goner!"

I didn't say much. "Oh, yeah, I'm all right. I had a great ride. But I wouldn't recommend the trip to a friend." I wasn't in much of a mood for talking.

The sun was beginning to set, and we had to get back home. In the gathering twilight we picked our way past that beautiful quiet pool at the foot of the foaming rapids. I paused a moment and gazed at the seemingly placid waters. A chill ran up my spine. I turned from the pool, looked up into the evening sky, and thanked my heavenly Friend for looking after one of His foolish children.

Deadman's Mine

by Kenn Sherwood Roe

F or years my friends and I had wandered around the ravines of Auburn Canyon in California. We had found gold pans, wagon wheels, ancient bottles, and even rusted revolvers. We knew the location of nearly every mine—we thought.

Then one day under a wooded ridge we found a hidden arroyo strewn with tailings and dirt debris from some long-forgotten mine. We discovered old winches, cables, and pulleys. And above, obscured by the thrust of an alder tree, was the mine opening. It was framed by crumbling earth and twisted beams. That alone should have been enough forewarning. But irresistibly drawn, we hunched over and stepped inside, the rush of stale air engulfing us. The opening, which led into a seemingly limitless dark void, proved larger than we expected, some eight feet high and seven feet wide.

"Wonder how far it goes," Norman said.

"Probably for miles," replied Gerry.

"Never knew a mine was here," said his twin, Ritchie.

"I wonder, I just wonder . . ." Norman repeated.

"Wonder what?" we chimed.

"I wonder whether this could be Deadman's Mine."

"*Deadman's Mine,*" we chorused in awe.

One popular legend claimed that two men had worked a rich vein using Chinese immigrants for cheap labor. The two had profited beyond all expectations. Then, mysteriously, one partner had vanished.

The lone inheritor had become progressively wealthier, flaunting his success with new carriages, fine horses, and stock in the local railroads. Suspicion had centered on him, and the rumors had spread. Apparently the mine played out shortly afterward, and he had disappeared, never to be heard of again.

According to several reports, the vanished miner, driven by greed, had murdered his partner. Local authorities had intended to look into the case, but the murky, formidable depths of the plunging shafts had discouraged thorough investigation. The mine was soon abandoned, then lost track of altogether. And so a legend found root to grow and survive, adding another colorful tale to a region rich in lore.

On the day we found the mine opening we saw a nearby stream splashing swiftly toward the river from some hidden spring high on the ridge. We followed the stream's laughing descent through lush growth to an abandoned stage road beside which stood a shack built of timber, rocks, slats, tar paper, tin, and mud. An old man sat outside, dozing in a broken rocker.

A hundred yards below the shack, where the river flowed cool and green, the man had piled rocks into a levee where he could pan gold in the quiet, trapped waters. He awakened with a start and regarded us suspiciously through a grizzled beard. Then his squinting eyes softened, and he invited us to join him on his porch.

We talked excitedly in the lengthening shadows. "Do you know anything about the old mine up there?" Norman asked, pointing up the hill.

"Only that it was mighty rich once," he replied, nodding as if to impress us of its great lost wealth.

"Could it be Deadman's Mine?" one of the twins asked.

He shrugged. "I've heard that story. I don't know. No one knows. But it well may be."

That night in my father's den my friends and I concluded that this was indeed the legendary mine! And we four high school students, exuberant and adventurous, were determined to explore the old mine shaft. A great mystery was soon to be solved. We envisioned the headlines: Local Boys Uncover Mystery. There would be a speech from the mayor; loud applause with people crowding about and reporters pushing them aside; a word from the governor; and certainly statewide—maybe even national—coverage. And possibly, just possibly, we might find a yet-untapped strain of gold rich beyond imagination!

And so we began planning, phoning, collecting our needed gear: knives, knapsacks, rope, flashlights, food, small rock picks. Knowing that our parents would object, we prepared in secret.

Finally one warm, spring-bright day we at last assaulted the mine. That day would live with me, haunt me, wake me years later in a sweat of fear and fantasy.

Linked to one another by heavy ropes—and equipped with flashlights, hard helmets, canteens, apples and cookies, and various apparatus—we cautiously wormed our way into the tunnel. Our enthusiasm waned momentarily as the bright opening disappeared from view, severing dramatically all connection with the outside world. I, the last of the four, felt the moment acutely, glancing back as a sour dampness enclosed us.

After hesitating a moment, we continued, held in a silent bond of determination and youthful daring. Down we penetrated into another era, the crude walls emerging weirdly in the flickering light.

Corroded candleholders still pricked the rocky walls, and an empty ore wagon lay overturned upon twisted rails. We found cables, a pick, and a shovel. To our amazement, the handles disintegrated into puffs of dust when we touched them. In a broken box we discovered bills and papers probably listing names or mining items. The ink had so faded on the moldy papers that they were impossible to read, but we recognized the swirly script that had been characteristic of the past century.

We turned to the right and followed along a gradual curve until the tunnel seemed to end, then rose abruptly in a 12-foot incline. Up we struggled against the loosening dirt.

"We could get lost," Ritchie said.

Undaunted, we pushed on, working slowly through the meandering route.

"I don't like this," Gerry admitted, expressing my own feelings.

But I withheld my thoughts, not wishing to appear scared. After all, they were seniors and I was a mere sophomore. "Oh, no!" I uttered once as we pushed farther into the cold unknown. All of us were afraid now; I could sense it. And still we were drawn forward like pieces of metal toward some magnetic force.

Our footsteps, our words, even our breathing echoed and reechoed through the vaultlike enclosure.

Into the bowels of the earth we wound along the remains of a dream quest where men had feverishly traced an artery of gold. Tired, mud-caked men toiling day after day in musty air where a dynamite blast or a splintered timber might entomb them. Entombment. Buried alive. The possibility shook me. Why hadn't we considered that before?

Again the tunnel ended, rose, then proceeded as before—this time at the top of a 20-foot shaft. An old pipe followed the ascent along one side to curve into the upper level.

"Guess this is the end of the line," Ritchie said.

"Guess it is," I quickly added.

"Maybe not," said Norman. "We can make it. We'll climb the pipe."

"Sure we can," said Gerry. "I'll go first."

And so we removed our connecting ropes.

This is stupid, I thought, not expressing my fears. By now Gerry was scaling the vertical wall, our lights upon him, his strong overhand reach carrying him into the next adventure. Behind him went his brother, Ritchie, less certain, his feet tumbling loose rubble as he hung dearly to the pipe, resting often after jerky starts.

Then came my turn. Determined, I struggled upward, my masculine image in jeopardy. Surprisingly, I rose strongly the first 15 feet. Then I faltered, struggled, felt my arm muscles tighten. With my whole body shaking, I inched higher by wrapping my legs around the pipe for support. Squirming hard, I managed a gradual advancement. A few feet short of the goal, I gave up. No effort, no encouragement, no degree of restful pause sufficed. I managed to cling helplessly in fear of falling.

"Try, you dumb bunny," Norman shouted.

Desperately, in a do-or-die effort, I pedaled at the tubelike shaft for footing, pummeling rocks and earth at him below. Throwing his arms across his face, he lurched sideways under a miniature avalanche. Miraculously, I felt myself carried aloft as Gerry and Ritchie somehow managed to reach the scruff of my jacket.

Norman followed too easily, his muscular arms and vicelike hands reaching out rhythmically. We sat chuckling in nervous release. Then silently we gulped our lunches. Our dim lights shone faintly against the crushing dark, little solace as we realized how deep in the earth we now were.

"What's this?" asked Ritchie, his hands groping some mushy, elongated objects. He held one up, thick and gummy in his palm. "Ugh," he snorted, tossing it away, back down into the hold from which we had emerged.

"Wait!" Norman cried. "It might explode!"

Stunned, we flashed the lights over the rounded pile he had encountered. Sure enough, an overturned box registered the unmistakable word: DYNAMITE. An entire box of explosives had been left there long ago; the sticks, which looked like enormous fire-crackers, had melted into one another, a glob of sticky powder and cardboard. We sat hushed, the impact registering slowly.

"Let's get out of here," Gerry managed, his voice cracking.

"OK," said Norman, picking up equipment.

Then came the most horrible sound one can experience—the nightmarish, whirring shrill of rattlesnakes just beyond in the black. We had awakened them from hibernation. The old mines are a natural place for snakes to slumber out the winter, interlocked and coiled in a mass. With the balminess of spring, they move slowly from their torpor to search for food. Old-timers know that; historians have recorded the fact; our biology teacher had described it. But here we were nearly in their bedroom, their sound filling the narrow confines with a reverberating roar. I visualized thousands of them slithering toward us, around us, over us.

"Let's go!" screamed Ritchie, grabbing the pipe to hurtle over the rim.

"Fool," yelled Norman. "You could start an avalanche."

Looking embarrassed, Ritchie leaned back against the wall.

"Gerry, hold your light on us and follow us down with it so we can see," Norman ordered. "Ritchie, you go first. I'll go next; then we'll hold the pipe steady for Kenn."

I appreciated Norman's commanding presence and his concern for me. Suddenly I felt a tremendous burden. I had to master myself. I could not fail them again. But I knew what they didn't; I hadn't rested long enough. My arms and shoulders still trembled, drained of energy.

Gerry squatted impatiently behind me; in the half-light I detected him shaking too. Ritchie and then Norman vanished over the edge, a beam of light flooding around. Cringing, I listened to the constant buzz of rattlers, now unbearably chilling.

"Come on, Kenn," came the inevitable words.

It'll be easy going down, I told myself. Clutching the pipe, I rolled over the ledge, the glaring flashlights blinding me, making everything whirl. I looked down to clear my eyes and to judge the distance. The 20-foot drop appeared more like 40. I froze, only to feel myself slipping, losing control, my grasp weakening.

"Hang on! Hang on!" someone shouted.

Frightened, I began kicking for support, for anything. Part of the sidewall gave way, slabs beside me peeling loose, then roaring and rumbling away. Vaguely I saw Ritchie and Norman below, their arms flailing, the rocks and exploding dirt spattering all over them. Ritchie fell backward, the debris pouring over his legs. Norman staggered and finally sprawled awkwardly.

Sliding helplessly and screaming wildly, I landed in a mound of mushy dirt. As the cascading soil diminished, Norman retrieved a flashlight and cast it over me and Ritchie, then up at Gerry, who stood rigid, as though uncertain of what had happened. The rush of gravel and sand slowed to silence, broken intermittently by the flush of soft dirt and accentuated by a crackle of rattlers farther back.

"You guys OK?" Gerry cried.

"Stay up there," Norman hissed, trying to hold his voice down. "It might start again."

For a long time we sat, stunned. Tears streamed down my face.

"Back out of his way," Norman finally said, pushing Ritchie and me away as Gerry shimmied down the pipe like a professional firefighter.

The way out was interminably long. We had left most of our equipment behind, and when a canteen dropped from Ritchie's knapsack, no one turned to pick it up. Twice we heard crumbling earth thundering, then fading into a murmur. Both times we stopped, held our breath, and fought an almost overwhelming urge to run, to burst away.

"Whole lousy place could come down," said Ritchie, his voice trembling, his eyes darting overhead.

"Shut up," Norman snapped.

Then directly before us rays of filtered light haloed a bend in the tunnel. Whooping with delight, Ritchie sped ahead. Perhaps foolishly, but uncontrollably, we followed. How beautiful was the sight of the opening, the brilliant sunlight. And the river below. And the sweetness of mountain air.

For me, there followed a father's reprimand and a mother's tears upon learning why we were late. And I was to pay plenty in the years following, waking in the night cold with sweat at the memory of the damp earth crashing about us. How precious is life! How much we owe to God for His protection!

Had we discovered Deadman's Mine? We will probably never know. But for us the name seemed fitting.

Other young explorers have not been so fortunate. They have died under tons of earth. For two decades now, as a ghost-town explorer, as a park ranger, as a member of rescue teams, I have tried to impress people with one warning—*never* explore an abandoned mine without an experienced guide. I know. I've been on forbidden ground!

18

Appointment With Death

by Maryane Myers

Driving past the white house nestled among some stores in his Texas town, Jer McDonald glanced at a large sign near the front door.

Madame La Zorla—Clairvoyant, Medium
Why be in doubt about your future?
She sees all, tells all!
Knock on Madame La Zorla's door today!

Sitting beside Jer in the car was his best friend, Pete, who said, "That's a dumb sign. If she's so smart, why does she live in such a beat-up old house? Looks like she can't even conjure up enough money to get it painted!"

Usually Jer would have instantly agreed. But he'd heard rumors that several of Madame La Zorla's predictions had been pretty accurate. Curiosity tempted him to ignore the arguments against spiritualism that he'd learned at home and church school.

With a toss of his head he turned to his friend. "Ever since we were little kids, I've thought Madame La Zorla was a witch or something spooky. But a few nights ago in Elsir's Pharmacy I overheard a couple of women talking about her. They said Madame La Zorla can help people in a lot of ways. She tells them what investments to make, where to find missing objects—things like that."

Pete's eyes narrowed. "The devil can give her that power!"

Jer ignored the argument. "One woman said her husband had lost a billfold with $200 in it. They searched the house, office, car—everywhere. Finally the wife went to Madame La Zorla. The fortune-teller told her exactly where to find the billfold—in her husband's bathrobe pocket."

Gravel crunched beneath the car wheels as Jer turned into Pete's driveway. He switched off the ignition, staring straight ahead.

Pete looked at him thoughtfully. "You aren't thinking of going to a fortuneteller, are you?"

"Don't be ridiculous!" Jer pushed Pete with an elbow. "Let's go inside and talk."

In the den the two teens settled into comfortable chairs. Suddenly Pete's face brightened. "Only two weeks till we'll be going away to college."

Jer looked out a window into the August sunshine. "I wonder if I'm doing the right thing." He sighed. "Do I want to waste four years of my life in college? Maybe I should get out into the business world instead."

Pete shook his head in disbelief. "You won't be wasting time in college. Only a few days ago you were saying that a good education is necessary to get the kind of job you're interested in."

"I know. I'm just tired of school right now, I guess."

It was dark when Jer left Pete's house. Slowly he drove down Main Street toward home. Madame La Zorla's illuminated sign seemed to reach out, more intriguing than ever.

"I'd like to know about my future," Jer whispered. "Maybe she could tell me what I should do with my life." He shoved away the nagging thought that prayer and advice from his parents would be better ways to handle the uncertainty he felt.

As he sat in the car, a little voice said, "Nobody will know; go on in."

Another voice came back with "Going into her house would put you on Satan's ground. Get out of here now!"

Jer argued aloud with his conscience. "She's helped other people. I won't stay long enough for anything bad to happen."

He parked the car and knocked on her front door.

A few moments later Madame La Zorla opened the door. Jer hurried inside, hoping that no one had seen him. He stood face-to-face with a short, rotund woman wearing a long black cotton dress. Layers of beads circled her thick neck and sparkled in the artificial light. Her jet-black shoulder-length hair seemed out of place with all the wrinkles on her plump face.

Suddenly the scent of Madame La Zorla's perfume seemed sickeningly strong blended with stale kitchen odors and musty old wallpaper. Gulping, Jer fumbled for the doorknob. "I've—I've got to go—I don't feel well."

Quickly the woman stepped between him and the door. Her smile was pleasant. "The hall is terribly hot and stuffy." She placed a firm hand on his arm. "Come into the séance room; it's cool there."

"Some other time." He tried to open the door.

Madame La Zorla pulled him away, still smiling. "You came here for a very important message. You must not go away without it." She walked to a door at the end of the hall and opened it. "Come in; sit down with me. Tell me your problem. I can help you."

There was something compelling about her voice. Jer shrugged and followed her.

The séance room was small and dimly lit. Jer sat down at the table under the feeble lightbulb and stared at the crystal ball.

The woman sat down across the table. "You made the right decision to come tonight. Let us look into your future."

Curiosity made him bold. "Can you really see things in this ball?"

Madame La Zorla nodded.

"Could I?" he asked.

"No." Her voice was a spooky whisper.

For several minutes she did not move nor speak. Then, to his surprise, her face seemed to take on the appearance of a plastic mask. Her fingers fluttered slowly as she began moving her hands around and over the crystal ball.

After more silence, she spoke in a slow, strained voice that did not resemble her own. "There is a young boy near you, very young; he is your brother. You do not have a sister." She paused a moment before continuing. "There is another boy who goes where you go most of the time. He is not as tall as you. He does not belong to your family, but he is like a brother to you."

The truth of her words sent a shiver rippling down Jer's spine. *She's just guessing,* he thought.

"You passed this house a few minutes ago and could not decide whether to come in. You want to know about your future. You want to know—" Her raspy tones grew thin and faded out.

She took a breath, regaining her voice. "You and

your friend plan to take a trip. There is a great building. I see many young people going in and out of it. He will go—you will not."

Excitement momentarily shook Jer. *So I'm not going to college,* he thought. He burst out, "I'd like to get into business, someplace where I can make a good salary right from the start, with lots of chances to be promoted."

"What would you like to do?"

He shook his head. "I'm not sure. I'm hoping you can tell me what would be best."

Madame La Zorla's hands moved again to the crystal ball. Outstretched fingers circled back and forth as if brushing away a dense film that hid his future. "There is darkness—you are calling for help," she whispered. "I see—" She began to moan as an expression of horror filled her eyes. Slowly she drew back and gazed at him.

Jer, who had been bending toward the fascinating crystal ball, instantly leaned away, holding his breath.

Again Madame La Zorla looked into the orb. Her face became pale and distorted. "No! Oh, no! Not this boy!" Madame La Zorla groaned in a hoarse whisper.

What could be that bad? he wondered, feeling his clasped hands grow wet and icy cold. "What is it?" he demanded.

Sorrowfully she looked at him. "You are going to die—soon."

The bluntness of her words shook him. *This is just an act. She's trying to scare me,* Jer thought. "You're putting me on," he said, trying to sound nonchalant.

Madame La Zorla shook her head. "There is no escape; I can't help you. You are going to die November 13."

A few minutes later Jer sat in his mom's old green Chevy in the shadow-filled alley outside Madame La Zorla's house. "You are going to die soon—November 13!" He repeated her words aloud. "How stupid I've been, thinking she could give me advice about my future. She and that spooky voice of hers!" Gritting his teeth, he turned on the ignition and headed home.

Jer went to bed early but soon woke up and relived the evening's scary events. Several times that night he drifted into a troubled sleep, only to wake with a sickening feeling of impending doom.

As the days passed, he couldn't get the fortune-teller's prediction out of his mind. He longed to talk with his parents and Pete about what had happened, but he couldn't bring himself to do it.

What's the use? he thought. *They'd only quote Bible verses I already know. Dad and Mom would probably pray and ask God to forgive me—as if I hadn't already asked Him a dozen times. I'm as bad as King Saul in the*

Bible. He knew he shouldn't go to a medium for help. He died for it the next day. And my time has been set too: November 13. Madame La Zorla said I couldn't escape no matter how hard I try.

One night Jer felt so desperate that he got out of bed, dressed, and slipped outdoors. Everything was dark except a pale streetlight on the corner. Suddenly he remembered the bus station a few blocks away.

"A bus can take me out of here, and I've got to escape!" he whispered. "Pete will have to go to college without me. I'm going to California instead."

Quickly he walked back into the house. *I can't wait for the morning bus; Mom and Dad would try to stop me,* he thought. Jamming a few things into a flight bag, he wrote a brief note and quietly left.

"I'm on my way to freedom," Jer muttered as he boarded the bus for Los Angeles.

In Phoenix he acquired a new seatmate. "I'm Roy," the stranger announced with a crooked smile. He had shaggy brown whiskers, a bushy mustache, and shoulder-length hair.

"I'm Web," Jer lied.

"Going to L.A.?"

Jer nodded. "Yeah, I hope to get a job there."

"My brother has one waiting for me. If you don't mind loading crates, you can work there too."

A few days later Jer was laboring beside Roy on a shipping dock. For a while Jer thought his new life was really exciting. He had fun visiting Disneyland and other places in southern California. But every time he remembered Madame La Zorla's prediction, he sank into depression.

One Sunday evening he went to his rented room and flopped down on the bed. "October 1," he sighed, glancing at the calendar. "November 13 isn't far away." A sickening feeling enveloped him.

Roy knocked on his door and flipped the light switch as he walked in. "Web, what's the matter with you, sitting in the dark?"

Jer ignored him.

"Aren't you going to Phil's with me?"

"No."

Roy sat down and looked thoughtfully at Jer. "You're in trouble. Would you like to talk about it?"

When Jer didn't answer, Roy took a newspaper from his pocket. "Want to hear what Dear Abby has to say?"

"No!"

Roy turned a couple pages. "Well, when's your birthday? I'll read your horoscope."

Instantly Jer jumped to his feet, grabbed the paper, crumpled it up, and trampled it underfoot.

Roy hurried to the door. "Don't get excited. There's nothing wrong with horoscopes," he mumbled.

Jer glared at him. "They're tricks of the devil. Satan will do anything to lead us away from God."

"Preacher man, I'm leaving," Roy said. "See you at work."

After he left, Jer started stuffing clothes into his flight bag. "I can't stay here a minute longer," he told himself. "My time is running out. I can't waste the days I have left."

Denver, Chicago, Pittsburgh were stops on a trail that ended in New York City. "Even death can't find me here with all these other people around," Jer thought aloud. For several days he felt comfortable. Then fear returned, stronger than ever. Madame La Zorla's words, "You can't escape," kept ringing in his ears.

One night in early November Jer wandered through a vast downtown throng. Cold sleet stung his face. He groaned, "Dear Jesus, I didn't trust You with my future. I turned away from Your great love and went to a medium instead."

A tear trickled down his cheek. "I knew I was breaking the first commandment—putting a fortune-teller before God. Now Satan controls me, and there's no peace for me anywhere."

He sobbed aloud. Nobody seemed to notice. "I'm doomed," he cried in a whisper. "I might as well go home to die."

It was November 9 when Jer knocked at his parents' door. The joyful welcome from his family failed to comfort him.

Tactfully his parents tried to find out why he'd run away from home. Finally on the night of the twelfth, Jer asked them to come to his bedroom. Tears filled his eyes as he told them everything. "I deliberately sinned when I went to Madame La Zorla's. I've told God that I'm sorry, but I don't feel that He hears me. I tried to run away from her prediction, and now I know that it can't be done."

Love and sympathy mingled in his dad's voice. "Jer, I agree that it was a mistake to go to a fortune-teller. But if you're truly sorry for it—and I'm sure you are—get on your knees and ask God's forgiveness. He won't fail you; give Him a chance."

Jer shook his head, trying hard to keep back tears. "I've begged to be forgiven. There's no answer. No hope."

His mom cried softly. Dad sat on the bed beside Jer and put his hand on the young man's shoulder. "Son, there are a few things you've forgotten. First, we have all sinned. 'There is none righteous, no, not one' [Romans 3:10, KJV]. Second, God promises to forgive anyone who asks. That's where faith comes in. Remember the verse you learned in Sabbath school? 'Let the wicked forsake his way, and the unrighteous man his thoughts: and let him return unto the Lord, and he will have mercy upon him' [Isaiah 55:7, KJV]."

Jer lifted his head. "I haven't been thinking of His

mercy, only my sins." His voice held a tinge of hope.

Dad nodded understandingly. Going to Jer's bookcase, he pulled out a small book. "Son, I want to read you something from page 51 of *Steps to Christ:* 'You cannot atone for your past sins; you cannot change your heart and make yourself holy. But God promises to do all this for you through Christ. . . . Do not wait to *feel* that you are made whole, but say, "I believe it; it *is* so, not because I feel it, but because God has promised."'"

Mom smiled at her son. "Jesus' promises are so sure that He sealed them with His own blood. Let's kneel and talk to Him now."

Their prayers were sincere and full of faith. Jer rose from his knees and smiled. "I believe that my sins are forgiven," he declared with confidence. "Tomorrow is *not* the last day of my life. Instead, it's the beginning of a better life."

"Praise God!" Dad said reverently.

The morning of November 14, Jer woke to the music of raindrops tapping against the windowpane. He hopped out of bed and looked outside. "Rain!" he exclaimed, as if it were the most perfect thing that could happen to a day.

Great peace filled him. "Thank You," he said to Someone who seemed very near. God's great love had given him new life.

19

Chet and the
Super Coop Scooper

by Maylan Schurch

Vrooommm! The back of his T-shirt warm with the afternoon sun, my brother Chet straddled the three-wheeled Davis chicken coop cleaner and revved the engine. "Hurry up, Herman," he muttered.

At 16, Chet was actually a bit young to be operating the Davis. But nobody else on the South Dakota egg farm wanted the job.

"Let Chet do it," they'd tell Herman, the assistant manager. "He gets a kick out of it."

And he did. The Davis was only half as big as a farm tractor, but it was fast. It had a boxlike bucket on the front, which rode low to the ground.

"Come on, Herman," Chet muttered louder, revving the engine again.

The older guys didn't like driving the Davis because of what it carried. The Davis existed for only one reason: to rapidly remove chicken waste from henhouses. Some days the manure was hard and sticky; other days it was sloppy. Every day it smelled. Chet, however, enjoyed driving the Davis so much that he simply held his breath a lot.

Blatt-blatt-blatt-blatt. An old red farm tractor with a front-loader scoop finally sputtered around the corner. "Ready?" called Herman.

Chet gave him the OK sign, gulped a breath of fresh air, grabbed the controls, and nosed the Davis out of the sunlight and into the dim, dusty atmosphere of the 200-foot-long chicken house.

Vroooommm! A long, wide aisle lay before him. Fixing his eye steadily on the nearest pile of manure, Chet bore down on it with the Davis, lowered the bucket, and hit the pile hard. *Squincchh.*

"Boy," murmured Chet, trying not to breathe, "today's a sloppy day." *Snarrrll.* Up went the bucket. *Rowwwrrr.* Backing out into the sunshine, Chet pivoted and dumped the smelly load, *splatchhh,* into Herman's big tractor scoop.

Herman grabbed a hydraulic lever and raised the scoop to a great height. By the time he put the tractor in gear and *blatt-blatted* forward, his front-loader towering and swaying high above him, Chet and the trusty Davis had dived back into the chicken house. Trying not to breathe, Herman quickly *glopped* his load onto a tall pile of chicken manure and then hurriedly backed up again, getting into position just in time to see Chet backing furiously out into the sunshine with another quantity of chicken effluvia.

Over the past couple months Chet and Herman had built up a pretty good rhythm. And today the rhythm was going better than ever. The Davis was eating voraciously into the nasty mess inside the chicken house. Herman's dumpings were causing the manure pile to grow to mountainous proportions. It looked as though the two guys would be finished with the job in record time.

But suddenly Herman lost concentration. After Chet dumped a load into his scoop, Herman let himself be distracted for a few seconds by something in the distance. And that threw everything out of sync.

And Chet never suspected what was coming.

Vrooommm. Inside the henhouse, roaring past the clucking fowls in their cages, Chet scooped up another wet slab of manure. Glancing back over his shoulder at the square of bright sunlight that was the door, he backed the Davis rapidly toward it. Once the sun was on his shoulders, he got ready to pivot—

Whummpp!

Something hard caught Chet under his left shoulder. Jolted breathless, he felt himself tumbling through the air. And then, Chet tells me, he landed. A soft, gentle landing. But that was the only thing good about it. Because once Chet had collected his senses and looked around, he found himself reclining waist-deep squarely in the center of Herman's reeking mountain of chicken manure.

Suddenly he heard the tractor's loud *blatt-blatt-blatt* come to a stop.

"Chet?" Herman's voice was hoarse and low. "Chet?"

My brother blinked and wiped at his face a little with one of his wrists. Bad move. The wrist was gloppier than his face.

"Chet? Are you all right?"

Chet nodded, still in a fog. "What happened?" he asked in a fuzzy voice.

"I don't know," Herman admitted. "I was just raising the scoop and moving ahead when all of a sudden I heard this thump, and there you were." He hiccuped nervously a couple times. "Sure you're OK? No broken bones? Can you walk?"

"I'm fine," Chet assured him. Cautiously he felt all over those portions of himself that weren't immersed in manure; then he began to try to work one leg loose from the gooey mass beneath him. And as Chet was struggling like a man in quicksand, Herman began to laugh.

He decently tried to conceal the first snort, but after that he gave up. He yelped and hooted and slapped both his legs, one after the other.

Chet stared sourly at the assistant manager from

beneath a thatch of chicken manure that had attached itself to his forehead. Then he looked around him, realized the absolute silliness of his condition, and burst into helpless laughter himself.

And as he rolled out of that manure pile he discovered that, because of a fairly major miracle, he was indeed fine. If Herman's tractor scoop had been raised just 12 inches higher, Chet would have caught it on the base of his skull, and he could have been paralyzed—or maybe killed.

But he was fine. Thanks to a deft, and probably smiling, guardian angel (one with a strong nose and an equally strong sense of humor), Chet was fine.

20

Voices in the Darkness

by Jane Chase

Hey, you in the tent. Is that your canoe by the boat ramp?"

I jerked awake and rolled over to face Wendy. I couldn't see my cousin in the darkness but knew she was awake.

The voice came again. "If that's your canoe, you're going to want to move it."

I sat up in my sleeping bag and answered, "Yeah, that's our canoe. Is something wrong?"

"Not really," the voice replied. "But it might get stolen if you leave it at the ramp."

"Um, just a sec." I turned to Wendy and whispered, "We've got to bring the canoe up."

"I know. I heard him," Wendy replied. "But I can't help carry the canoe. I twisted my ankle this afternoon, remember?"

"Do I dare go out there alone?" I whispered. "What if he's a murderer or something?"

Wendy sat up and put on her glasses. "But what if someone takes the canoe? My dad will kill me. That guy's a park ranger. He won't do anything."

I had to decide quickly. The man was waiting for an answer. Meeting him might be dangerous, but facing Wendy's father if the canoe was stolen would be dangerous too.

"I can bring your canoe up in the back of my truck if you want," the man offered.

I decided to take a chance. "OK," I called out, "I'm coming." I pulled on my jeans and shoes.

We heard the rumble of the man's truck pull up outside the tent. I took out my Marine Corps fighting knife and clipped the leather sheath to my belt. Until now I had used it for only such things as pounding tent pegs and digging fire pits. I hoped I wouldn't have to use it to defend myself.

I slipped out of the tent into the black night. Beyond the picnic table a dark pickup truck stood idling. I took a deep breath and marched toward it.

When I opened the door, the man said, "Hi. I wondered if you were coming."

"It takes longer to get dressed in the dark," I answered as I climbed into the cab.

The man chuckled. "Yeah, I guess so." He put the truck in gear, and it lurched forward. "I'm Greg," he said. "I take care of this place during the summer."

He glanced at me and went on. "I left my boat down at the ramp a couple weeks ago, and someone took the motor. That's why I thought it would be best not to leave a canoe down there."

"Yeah." I tried to relax, remembering the Bible verse that said, "For he will command his angels concerning you to guard you in all your ways" (Psalm 91:11). I knew that with God protecting me, everything would be all right.

Greg seemed nice. I guessed he was in his 20s. He had a rugged face and light hair that looked greenish in the light from the dash panel.

While he drove, Greg talked about his job at the park. I tried to listen, but the farther Greg drove, the more frightened I became. Our campsite wasn't *that* far from the lake. Then I realized that Greg wasn't taking me to the lake. He was taking me into the woods. I had to escape.

I slipped my hand to the hilt of my knife and pulled it from its sheath. Holding it at my right side, out of sight, I prayed, "God, give me courage." Then I pivoted left, swung the knife out, and brought the steel blade up under Greg's jaw. "Stop the truck," I commanded.

Greg's eyes widened, and he slammed on the brakes. The truck slid to a halt. "What are you doing?" he asked.

"Take me back." My hand shook, and I tried to steady it.

"I'm not kidnapping you," Greg said. "There are trees down on the road, and we have to go around." He seemed sincere. I didn't know what to think.

Greg's hand darted out. He grabbed my wrist. With a wrench he pulled my arm back and snatched the knife.

He slid the truck's gearshift to park and leaned toward me, the knife extended. I lunged back against the door. He was going to kill me.

My mind felt numb. My stomach lurched. All I could think of was God, *help me, God, help me.*

A voice floated into the back of my mind. *Open the door.*

I realized that my hand was resting on the door latch. I pushed down hard on the handle, fell backward out of the cab, and quickly scrambled *under* the truck.

I heard Greg curse as he crawled across the seat after me. He'd find me any minute.

Take the truck. It was that same voice, echoing in my mind. The truck was running; he'd left the keys in the ignition.

With my heart in my throat, I slid out from underneath the truck, yanked open the driver's door, and jumped in. I threw the gearshift into drive and stamped on the accelerator. The truck leaped forward. I'd just gotten my driver's license that spring, and it was all I could do to keep the truck on the winding road. I kept driving, not sure where our campsite was.

Relief flooded me as I rounded a corner and saw our tent. I pulled into the campsite and jumped out of the truck.

"Wendy, come on, we've got to go!" I yelled as I scrambled into the tent.

"What happened?" Wendy asked.

"It's Greg—that man. He tried to kidnap me!" I grabbed my clothes and sleeping bag, bundling them up as fast as I could. "I've got his truck. If we hurry, we can beat him to the boat ramp."

We drove to the ramp. Wendy hobbled to the canoe, flipped it right side up, and took our gear as I unloaded it. I held the canoe steady as Wendy climbed in and clambered to the bow.

"Hurry!" she yelled. "Here he comes!"

I glanced back and saw Greg racing down the trail toward the beach. I gave the canoe a shove. It floated free.

"Hurry!"

Greg splashed into the water behind me. I swung one foot into the canoe and pushed off with the other. Hands grabbed my ankle. I fell into the canoe, twisted my body, and kicked free.

Wendy paddled the canoe out of his reach. Greg

waded deeper in the water, but the canoe outdistanced him. His curses followed us.

We kept paddling. Greg's voice faded until we couldn't hear him anymore. The shoreline looked like a long, black snake on the horizon. I finally relaxed, and we let the canoe drift. The only sound was the water dripping from the paddles.

"I've never been so scared in my life," I said softly, holding back tears. "I thought he was going to kill me."

"How did you get away?" Wendy asked.

"Well, I heard a voice telling me what to do." I laid my paddle across my knees. "Do you think that God talks to people that way? that He says things like 'Open the door' and 'Take the truck'?"

"God can say anything He wants," Wendy replied. "But the person He's talking to has to be listening to hear Him."

"Maybe so." I was glad I had listened to the Voice. It saved my life.

Farm Girls on the Run

by Judy McEvoy

Hey, Judy! Grandpa said not to go in there," my older sister reminded me. "The new bull has horns 10 inches long and is really mean."

"Come on, Brianna," I urged. "Nothing's going to happen. The bull's way over on the other side of the pasture."

She cautiously looked around before following me through the gate. The "back 40" acres on our farm were mostly grass except for a little patch at the bottom of the hill. There trees and brush grew thick alongside a stream. That's where we were headed.

We started toward the stream with our dog, Ted, tagging along behind. We followed the winding cow path down the hill. After a couple of minutes I heard Brianna hiss, "He sees us!"

"Forget it, Brianna. We're halfway there," I

pointed out. "If he comes toward us, we'll run to the trees. It's safe there."

I glanced at the bull a few times, but I didn't really pay much attention until I heard Brianna shriek.

"What?" I asked, turning around.

"The—the bull!" she stammered. "We can't reach the trees."

She didn't have to explain. I could see that the bull had eased around, cutting us off from the trees—and safety.

I looked behind us. We were a long way from the fence. "We've got to go back." I gulped. "It's our only chance."

Brianna started walking backward very slowly. "Walk the same way we were already walking so he won't know we're scared," she whispered.

It sounded like good advice. But when we started walking, the bull started running. Have you ever seen 800 pounds of pure muscle hurling itself toward you? One look was enough for me.

My feet barely touched the ground as I ran. Yet every time I looked around, the bull was closer. Soon I head the bull behind me. I glanced back, and my heart almost stopped. Not only was the beast a mere 20 feet behind me, but he had lowered his head to the ground. He was closing in, ready to toss me to the moon.

I was out of breath from running, but I managed

to beg "Please, help me, God!" again and again. I was so terrified that that was all my brain could think, but I figured God knew what I needed.

The bull's thundering hooves on the hard ground sounded like drumbeats as he got closer and closer. Then I heard Brianna screaming over the hoofbeats, "Run, Judy, run!"

Brianna beat me to the fence. Kneeling in the two-foot-deep ditch, she held up the bottom strand of barbed wire. "Slide!" she screamed. "*Slide!*"

I dove headfirst for the empty space between the ground and wire. The next thing I knew I was lying on my back in the ditch with Brianna lying next to me. My heart was pounding like the hooves of cattle in a stampede.

"Don't move," Brianna cautioned. The bull stuck his head and neck through the top two strands of wire. His weight was stretching the wire so tight that his body was tilted over the ditch.

"He can't see us," Brianna whispered. "Lie still—and pray."

I couldn't have gotten up if I'd wanted to. The bull's nose was so close to my face that I could feel his breath. I prayed for help.

Everything became really quiet except for the bull's snorts. His nose twitched as he sniffed the air. Just when I thought the wire was going to snap from the bull's weight, I heard a loud growl.

I had forgotten about Ted, but it was a good thing that he hadn't forgotten us. He charged the bull's front leg and bit it. It took Ted three tries, but the bull finally forgot us and attacked him.

I sat openmouthed, gasping each time the bull's horns missed hooking Ted by inches. Brianna jumped up, grabbed my arm, and yelled, "Let's get out of here! Over there, to the cornfield!" A couple of minutes later we scrambled to safety.

We turned to see Ted. The bull was tossing his head wildly as he charged at the dog.

"Ted!" I shouted. "Come here!" Brianna joined me in calling him. We whistled his special "Come here" whistle and yelled as loud as we could. "Hurry, Ted, run!"

When he saw that we were safe, he scooted under the fence and ran toward us. The three of us ran as fast as we could to the house. It felt great to collapse on the grass in the yard.

I threw my arms around Ted and gave him a big hug. Then I whispered, "Thanks, God."

I'd never thought a farm could be dangerous. Of course, if I had listened to Grandpa, it wouldn't have been.

Miracle in the Mist

by Jonelle M. Brody

Don't forget your life jacket," Mother had advised.

Roger Woodward exhaled loudly, annoyed as he recalled her warning. *Why does it always have to be me?* he wondered, eyeing his sister and the other empty vest beside her. No one was making Deanne put on *her* life jacket.

Another one of those teenager things, he reasoned miserably, fastening the adult-size vest around his child-size frame. *I can't wait until I'm a teenager.*

"All ready?" Jim Honeycutt's voice interrupted Roger's self-pity.

"Ready!" exclaimed Deanne.

Roger smiled and allowed his frustrations to fade away. How could he stay upset? It was a beautiful July day, and he was going on his very first boat ride.

Ever since his family had moved from Greensburg, Pennsylvania, to Sunny Acres in upper New York, Roger had often marveled at the waters. But his dad's friend, Mr. Honeycutt, would be the first person to actually take him and his sister out in them.

Mr. Honeycutt started the motor and steered the 12-foot aluminum vessel out into the river. They were off!

As they rode along, Deanne chatted easily with Mr. Honeycutt while Roger took in the sights. He hung his fingers over the side of the boat and let them skim the waves. The water was cool—what a relief! He had worn only his swimsuit, and the afternoon sun burned his skin.

Roger lifted his dripping hand from the water and shook it in Deanne's direction.

"Hey!" she shrieked.

Mr. Honeycutt chuckled, and Roger turned his attention to an approaching bridge.

Are we going under it? Roger wondered eagerly. Yes, they were!

Roger's face lit up as they passed under the Grand Island Bridge, and he examined the underbelly of the structure. No young person he knew had *ever* said they'd done this before. Just wait until he told his parents about it!

Feeling upbeat and lighthearted, Roger wanted to wave a cheerful greeting to some boaters on the adjoining island, but something in their faces made him hesitate. Instead, he said nothing as they stared at him in awe.

Mr. Honeycutt navigated toward a park along the bank. But as they passed a shoal, the engine hit a rock, damaging one of the boat's safety devices. The engine roared. The seagulls screeched. Suddenly Mr. Honeycutt could not control the boat, and they began to pick up speed.

Roger's fingers curled around the side of the boat. He watched Mr. Honeycutt's face turn pale as he shut off the engine and grabbed an oar in each hand.

"Get into that vest," Mr. Honeycutt directed Deanne. He quickly glanced at Roger, then turned his focus to the swells.

But try as he might, Mr. Honeycutt could not gain any leverage in the swift currents.

The first wave hit the back of the boat. Just as Deanne fastened her vest, a second wave flipped them over completely.

Roger's head hit something—hard—and for a few seconds he became disoriented. After a moment, though, he found himself being thrown to and fro like a rag doll among the rocks.

Roger could not see Deanne or Mr. Honeycutt. He knew only that he was being dragged toward a thundering cloud of mist a short way ahead.

Deanne tried to hang on to the overturned boat,

but it hurt her hand to hold on to the rim. Finally the churning waters forced her to let go. Deanne's only hope was to try to swim to shore.

On nearby Goat Island a group of tourists watched incredulously as a boat went by, headed straight toward the falls. Only one of them, John Hayes, sensed that something was wrong.

Whose boat is this? he pondered.

Hayes looked around in the Niagara River and glimpsed Deanne struggling to get to the embankment.

"Girl, swim to me!" Hayes screamed.

Deanne could not see her rescuer—she only heard his voice—and it gave her the encouragement she needed.

Hayes climbed over the railing and reached out his hand to Deanne. She missed. But in her second attempt she caught Hayes by the thumb.

The onlookers stood stunned. Fortunately John Quattrochi, another tourist, realized that Hayes would surely lose his hold on the girl in those strong waters. So Quattrochi also sprang into action. Together he and Hayes pulled Deanne to safety, 20 feet from the crest of Niagara Falls.

Once on land Deanne, exhausted and distraught, frantically told the others about her brother and Mr. Honeycutt.

Quattrochi nervously whispered, "Pray for them."

Meanwhile Roger continued to bounce in the rapids. *What should I do?* he speculated desperately.

He couldn't swim—he'd never learned how. He peered around anxiously and spied several people running up and down the riverbank, pointing at him. *Why won't they rescue me?* he asked himself, his panic turning to anger.

Although Roger still had no idea what lay ahead, he began to accept that he was going to die in the river that afternoon. He thought of his family and his dog. He even considered what his parents might do with his toys.

Suddenly everything went dark.

Roger doesn't remember catapulting out into the cloud over Horseshoe Falls. He doesn't recall the 170-foot drop where more that a half million gallons of water surge over the edge every second. He has no recollection of landing in the mist pool, miraculously missing every single one of the tons of boulders that lie in wait at the base.

All he knows is that when he awoke from his daze, a ship had appeared.

The "ship" was a tour boat called *Maid of the Mist*. One of the crew spotted Roger's bright-orange life jacket bobbing like a cork in the haze. Roger waited as Captain Keech maneuvered the boat toward him.

It took three attempts before Roger could get ahold of the round life preserver. He was finally pulled aboard.

Then, ironically, yet to everyone's relief, he innocently cried, "May I have a cup of water?"

Roger and his sister were examined at local hospitals. Amazingly, Deanne had only a few cuts and scrapes, and Roger suffered from a bruise on his head.

Since he wasn't wearing a life jacket, no one saw Mr. Honeycutt's tussle in the rapids. They didn't see him go over the falls, either. But his body was found four days later, far down the river.

Many people spend their entire lifetime searching for God. But Roger Woodward met Him as a young boy. In a miracle. In the mist. There the Lord's mighty hand caught him and delivered him from danger.

If anyone asks him how he survived, he will answer, "It wasn't the hand of fate, nor the hand of luck, nor the spirit of Lelewala [the "maid of the mist" in Native American legend]. It was the Spirit of the living God who saved our lives that day and gave us hope that one day my sister and I would come to know Him."

23

Never Alone

by Richard Edison

Frank's thumb was turning blue. In fact, his whole body felt like an icicle.

The cold wind tore at his jacket. He'd been hitch-hiking for hours, and all he'd gotten for his efforts were two short rides and a frozen thumb. He was beginning to wonder if he might freeze to death on this desolate stretch of highway in eastern Washington.

At least I'm not alone, Frank thought. Through chattering teeth Frank prayed, "God, all I want to do is get home for Christmas. This morning I asked You to protect me and impress the right people to pick me up. Thank You for the rides I've had, but Lord, it's been a long time since the last one, and I'm freezing. Please send someone soon." Immediately Frank felt better—not warmer, but definitely better.

Moments later a car pulled over. With a silent

prayer of thanks Frank climbed in, the warmth from the car's heater surrounding him like a wool blanket.

"So, where you headed, bud?" The slurred words and overpowering stench of alcohol on the other passenger's breath sent a wave of apprehension through Frank. The driver didn't look much better, with bloodshot eyes and a disturbing tendency for looking at everything except the road ahead.

What have I gotten myself into? Frank thought. For a moment he considered asking to be let out, but the pleasant warmth of the car's heater, combined with the memory of the cold roadside, made him change his mind.

"H-home for Christmas break," he stammered in answer to the passenger's question.

"College man, huh? Where at?"

"I'm studying for the ministry at Walla Walla College."

"You must be a Seventh-day Adventist. My folks are Adventists. Good ones, too. Go to church on Saturday, don't eat meat, don't dance—all that stuff. Me, I ain't never seen where religion did anyone much good. Even used to date an Adventist girl. She tried to get me to walk the straight and narrow, but I never could get the hang of it. Guess I was just born to be wild. Right, Roy?" The man roared with laughter at his joke and slapped the driver on the back, causing him to swerve momentarily into the other lane.

"Oh, yeah. You're a wild man, Greg." The driver growled. "Now stop hitting me and let me drive."

"Just shut up, Roy. No wonder I was the pilot and you were the copilot. You don't drive any better than you fly—"

Sensing an opportunity to keep the older man busy so that Roy could concentrate on driving, Frank interrupted: "So, Greg, were you guys pilots in the war or something?" World War II had ended just four years earlier.

"Yeah, we were pilots. Flew bombers together on 54 raids over China, Burma, and India. Best pilots they had. Not that they'd ever admit it," he ended sullenly. Taking another swig from the whiskey bottle he held, Greg lapsed into a rare silence, staring vacantly into the night.

After a few minutes Roy spoke up. "Come on, Greg. You gotta let it go. Ain't nothin' we can do about the government and how they treated us. Besides, we ain't doin' that bad."

"What do you mean, we ain't doin' that bad? No jobs, this dumpy car, drivin' around trying to scrape up enough money for gas. We're heroes! Heroes, I tell you, and they shuck us aside like so much garbage! 'Mentally unstable,' they said. Yeah, right. We'll show them mentally unstable tomorrow."

"Shut up, man!" Roy hissed. "We ain't alone, remember?"

"Oh, yeah," Greg muttered. "Guess I forgot." Turning, he stared at Frank as if he were seeing him for the first time. Then he smiled. "Going to be a minister, huh? Maybe you should study psychology instead and help messed-up guys like us. What do you think of that?"

For a second Frank thought he heard a genuine plea for help behind the man's sarcastic tone, but then, with a curse, Greg turned back to his bottle. The three travelers fell into an uneasy silence, each lost in their own thoughts.

A short time later as they were approaching the town of Arlington, Washington, Roy broke his silence. "If you pay for some gas," he said to Frank, "we'll take you all the way to Portland, Oregon."

No way I'm letting them get a look in my wallet, Frank thought. "No, this is OK for now," he replied aloud. "Why don't you let me out here?"

"Suit yourself, buddy. Good luck."

Moments later Frank found himself standing in the cold on a deserted section of the highway, watching his ride speed away around the next curve.

"Thank You, God, for getting me out of there," Frank prayed. "Now please impress someone else to give me a ride."

Over the next 45 minutes several cars sped past. They would slow momentarily on seeing Frank's outstretched thumb, but then they'd speed away. The cold seemed to be burrowing its way through the layers of clothes he wore. Tucking his chin down into his coat collar, Frank began to jog in place, trying to keep the blood flowing to his frozen limbs.

Lifting his head to the dark sky, Frank pleaded, "Please, Lord. Send me a ride! Any ride."

The words were barely out of his mouth when another car rounded the curve. Quickly Frank raised his frozen thumb, only to let it drop immediately when he recognized the vehicle. It was the same men who had given him a ride earlier.

The car pulled up beside him, and the sour stench of alcohol wafted through the cold night air from the open window.

"You still here? Well, hop in."

The door swung open, and a blast of warm air hit Frank in the face. He hesitated. He didn't want to go with them, but he knew he'd freeze to death if he didn't get out of the cold soon. With a resigned sigh Frank climbed in and pulled the door shut behind him.

As the car swerved back onto the highway, Frank saw Greg looking at him, a wicked grin on his face. "I think I'll get me another quart of whiskey," Greg said, reaching into the back. When his hand came back over the seat, Frank's eyes widened in horror. Instead of a whiskey bottle, Greg clutched a silver-plated automatic gun. Ramming the weapon into

Frank's ribs, he growled, "Glad to see us, Frank? We're sure glad to see you, aren't we, Roy?"

"Oh, yeah, real glad." Roy laughed and punched the accelerator, sending the car rocketing down the deserted highway into the black night.

As the gun poked into his ribs, Frank felt the blood drain from his face. Every muscle tensed, ready to help him flee, but he found he couldn't move. Besides, the way Roy was driving—squealing around curves and flooring it on the straightaways—it would have been foolish to jump out. Instead Frank sat frozen in his seat, thinking again and again, *I'm going to die; I'm going to die.*

"I'm going to blow you away, man! I've killed plenty of people, and I won't have no problem doin' you neither." The evil gleam in Greg's eyes told Frank he meant what he said.

Frank decided to try to keep the men talking. They were drunk, after all, and maybe if he kept them busy, they'd forget about killing him. "Aw, come on now, guys; this is no way to treat a fellow veteran. What do you want? I've got a suit in this case and five dollars in my wallet. I've got a checkbook, too, if that's any good to you."

"We don't want your money, and we don't believe you're no veteran neither," sneered Greg. "You don't talk like no GI, that's for sure. You don't swear, and you don't even like guns."

"Of course I don't like guns, especially when I've got one poking me in the ribs! Besides, I was a medic in the war. I didn't carry a gun. Here, I can prove it." Frank took out his wallet and handed Greg his old medic pass.

It took a moment for Greg's alcohol-befuddled brain to process the words on the pass, but then he mumbled, "Well, what do you know. He is a vet. Look, Roy."

After Roy examined the pass, he gave it back to Frank. The men's whole attitude seemed to change suddenly. Roy said, "Well, since you're a fellow GI and a buddy, I guess we'll let you go. We were going to kill you, slit you down the middle so you wouldn't float, and toss you in the river up ahead, but now we'll just let you out."

"That's right," Greg agreed, slapping Frank on the back. "Us soldiers gotta look out for each other. Besides, we really don't want to bother with little guys like you. We're looking for a big job. We've even got two machine guns in the back. Wanna see them?"

Frank shook his head. The last thing he wanted to see was any more guns. One per day was more than enough.

"Since you're such a good guy and a fellow GI, we'll drop you off near the next town. But you gotta promise not to turn us in, OK?" Greg winked at

Frank as if they were old friends.

Frank had a sudden vision of the two men bursting into a bank, guns blazing. He knew he couldn't let that happen just to save his own hide. He couldn't promise not to turn them in.

His voice shaking, he replied, "You fellows had better let me out here, where you'll have plenty of room to get away."

Roy slammed on his brakes and swerved to the shoulder, shouting, "We've gotta get rid of this guy!"

"OK, buddy. Have it your way," Greg said to Frank, his voice eerily calm. "Get out slowly and march out in front where we can see you. Don't look back, and no sudden moves."

As Frank got out of the car he could feel the gun pointed at his back. He was sure that these were his last moments on earth. Looking across the Columbia River, its north bank barely visible in the pale moonlight, Frank waited for the bullet to tear through his flesh.

Suddenly the car door slammed, and he heard gravel spraying up behind him. Moments later he was alone again by the side of the highway. Alone and alive!

Frank saw a farmhouse up ahead and headed in that direction. Although it was past midnight, the owners were outside telling their guests goodbye. One look at the terror in Frank's eyes was all it took to allay any suspicions they had about his story. They told him later that he'd never be that white again until he was dead.

The people called the police in the next town, The Dalles, Oregon. More than an hour later a patrol officer finally arrived and took Frank into town, dropping him off at the bus depot. The officer didn't seem to want to know anything about two drunk, mentally unstable men with machine guns. Frank thought, *He probably hopes they'll just head on down the road and someone else will have to deal with them. Trying to take on two men with machine guns is a good way for a small-town cop to get himself killed.*

His assailants had kept Frank's five dollars, so he tried to get the bus depot to take a check. He'd had enough hitchhiking for a lifetime! The bus clerk called the police to check on his story. "There's been no such crime reported," the police desk sergeant said. "Keep him talking till we get there."

A short time later Frank found himself in a dark jail cell. *This is crazy,* he thought. *Lord, what is going on? I'm not the criminal. I'm the victim!*

Finally, in the morning, the police made some calls and discovered that Frank's story was true. They let him go, but he was still stranded in a strange town with no money to get home. Reluctantly he headed for the highway and stuck out his thumb again.

Soon a truck driver headed for Portland picked

him up. He was a big, friendly man, and he looked at Frank with concern as Frank climbed into the truck cab. "Man, you shouldn't be hitchhiking on this road. There are some bad characters out here. You could get yourself killed."

"Yeah, tell me about it," Frank sighed, buckling himself in.

And all the way to Portland that's just what the truck driver did, every few miles pointing out another spot where someone had been murdered during the 16 years he'd been driving that route.

That night, safe in his bed at home, Christmas carols playing softly in the background, Frank thought again about how close he'd come to dying alone beside that deserted highway. But then he realized that he hadn't really been alone after all. His Best Friend had been with him all along. Tears streaming down his face, he quietly prayed, "Thank You, God. With You in my life, I'm never alone."